Live
NOW

Maureen Gaffney

The Way we Live NOW

Gill & Macmillan

Gill & Macmillan Ltd
Goldenbridge
Dublin 8
with associated companies throughout the world
© Maureen Gaffney 1996
0 7171 2150 X
Index compiled by Helen Litton
Print origination by The Unlimited Design Co., Dublin
Printed by ColourBooks Ltd, Dublin

A catalogue record for this book is available from the
British Library.

3 5 4 2

Contents

Women and Men

Acknowledgments

My grateful thanks to Conor Brady, Editor of *The Irish Times*, who first invited me to write these articles; to Patsy Murphy, Weekend Editor, who cheerfully provided me with every assistance and support; and most especially, to Caroline Walsh, Features Editor, who coaxed, chided, encouraged and persuaded me to believe that I could fit being a columnist into an already-crowded life. Without her support, these articles would never have been written.

Childhood

and

Adolescence

Going on a Temperamental Journey

We do not come into this world psychologically naked, although, as American paediatrician William Carey once remarked, 'Nobody seems to believe in temperament until they have their second child.' As early as nine minutes of age, many aspects of a baby's temperament are already detectable and will remain quite stable as the child gets older. Temperament is that basic disposition we are born with that shapes how we act and react, a kind of fundamental dynamic in our relationship with the world. From the first days of life, babies differ from each other in many ways:

> **Activity level.** Some babies are active, even before they are born. They kick vigorously in the womb, wriggle in their cots, and, once on their feet as toddlers, never walk when they can run. Other babies are much less active.
>
> **Regularity.** Babies differ in how regular their cycles are. Some eat, sleep and defecate at regular and predictable times. Others are very erratic.
>
> **Approach to novelty.** Some babies revel in anything new, approaching the world with gusto. Others seem to dread novelty.
>
> **Adaptability.** Some babies adjust quickly to change in their routine. Others become distressed at every minor disruption.
>
> **Intensity of reaction.** Some babies bring the house down when they laugh or cry. Others are more low-key, smiling when they are happy and whimpering only when they are sad.
>
> **Level of awareness.** Some babies react to the slightest sound, sight or touch; the least thing will disturb their sleep. Others seem unaware of loud noise, bright lights or even dirty nappies.

Mood. Some babies seem to be almost always in a sunny mood. Others are grouchy, miserable and prone to complain.

Distractibility. Some babies are easily distracted; a game may be enough to keep their minds off their hunger, at least temporarily. Others are relentlessly single-minded.

Attention span. Some babies play contentedly with one toy for a long time. Others flit from one toy or activity to another.

By the time babies are a few months old, their personality seems to have coalesced around these temperamental characteristics, particularly in terms of their levels of activity, sociability and fearfulness, and these remain remarkably stable throughout their lives. Very similar aspects of temperament can be identified in adults as well. Studies that tracked people over a long period have isolated three basic characteristics which stay stable right throughout life and form an enduring core to the personality: openness to new experiences (i.e. seeing change as an opportunity rather than as a threat, and a willingness to change your mind, or even your life, when it's necessary); fearfulness (i.e. having a low threshold for threat and needing a long time to recover from stress); and extroversion (i.e. a tendency to be outgoing, active and assertive).

Does temperament matter? Yes, to some extent. In a general way, temperament can act as a protective or a risk factor in how the child fares in the family and the wider world. Based on different combinations of the nine characteristics listed above, about 40 per cent of infants are classified as easy, about 15 per cent as slow-to-warm-up, and about ten per cent as difficult. The rest show mixed patterns. While many aspects of temperament seem to be largely innate, what is changeable is the expression of these characteristics. The task for parents is to help their child to find a better way to express and live with his or her particular temperament.

From the parent's point of view, it is useful to think of temperament as affecting the child's capacity to do two critical things: first, to maintain equilibrium, that is, not to become physiologically or psychologically disorganised in the face of novelty or threat; and second, to derive enough security from the presence of the care-giver to enable the child to explore and manage the world. To help the child maintain equilibrium, the parent's task is to adjust the amount of stimulation which the baby receives to his or her temperament. To enable the child to venture forth into life with confidence, the task is to find a reliable way to respond to and comfort the child, especially when it is distressed.

Managing the level of stimulation, in turn, depends on responding accurately and sensitively to the baby's signals. A sensitive parent will pick up, 'read' and adjust to the infant's signals. For example, when playing with the baby, the parent will intensify the stimulation (e.g. tickling, vocalising) when the baby smiles, maintains their gaze or reaches towards them, but will reduce or stop the action when the baby turns away or frowns. That in turn will allow the baby to control the amount of stimulation, to allow the right time for the build up of excitement and to 'recover' from the physiological disorganisation of too much stimulation, such as tickling. These tiny actions on the part of the baby are signals of his or her particular temperamental needs.

Similarly, comforting has to be attuned to the child's temperament. Slow-to-warm-up babies may need an exceptional amount of physical contact and protection from the unwanted intrusions of the world. Just as during pregnancy, the mother digested nutrition and 'fed' it to her unborn child, she now has to continue, for the first few months of the baby's life to 'digest' experiences and feed them back in a safe way to her timid baby. Difficult babies may look as if they do not want to be cuddled. But this is not so. Rather, their low tolerance for stimulation and their difficulty in recovering from frustration or upset make them extremely sensitive to any physical intrusion. In fact, because of their high internal irritability, they have a desperate need for physical comfort. The critical thing for the parent is to offer such comfort in response to a reliable cue from the child.

The biggest problems with temperament, however, tend to arise not from having a baby whom other people might describe as 'easy' or 'difficult', but from having a baby whom the particular parent finds difficult. The baby may not have a temperament that suits the parents. Some parents find it a joy to rear active babies who love stimulation and novelty, who loudly express their wishes and reactions. Other parents find it exhausting. Some parents may be delighted with a passive, timid baby with regular habits. Others may be disappointed.

While there is some evidence that difficult babies are at a higher risk of forming insecure attachments, it is not conclusive. Most parents seem to succeed in accommodating to and bonding with even the most challenging of temperaments. A baby is not a piece of putty to be moulded to the shape of the parent's fantasy. Rather, it is more useful to approach a child's temperament as the sculptor approaches the material to be worked on, adapting his craft to the particular properties of marble, wood or stone, allowing it to reveal its nature. Or to borrow another artistic analogy from the psychoanalyst Alfred Adler: the child is the artist as well as the painting.

Self-esteem in Childhood

I'm pretty sure of myself.
I'm an easy person to like.
I'm proud of my schoolwork.
I can usually handle things.
I'm popular with kids my own age.
My parents usually take my feelings seriously.
Things don't usually bother me.
Other kids like to follow my ideas.

I find it very hard to talk in front of the class.
I often wish I were someone else.
I don't care what happens to me.
I give in very easily.

These are examples of statements which are used to measure self-esteem in children; they give some indication of children's private experience of how it feels to have confidence or to lack it. They also illustrate the four different components of self-esteem: power, significance, virtue and competence. Power is the ability to influence and control others. Significance is the acceptance, attention and affection of others. Virtue is being good, adhering to certain moral standards. Competence is meeting the demands for achievement in the different spheres of one's life.

Somewhere between the ages of eight to ten, a child's self-esteem tends to stabilise. The developmental process begins at about age three when the child begins to acquire a sense of being a separate individual — of having an inner, private psychological self. Self-esteem is the gradual process of building up an evaluation of that self.

Children first define themselves in terms of their physical

appearance, then later in terms of their skills, their likes and dislikes, their psychological attributes. Most important, they begin to understand how they are seen by other people, particularly their parents, their friends, their teachers. They develop what is called a 'looking-glass self' — an internal reflection of how they have been viewed and treated by those who are important to them — their parents, wider family, friends, teachers. If they are treated with respect and love, they come to believe that they are worthy of respect and love. What was once done to them by their parents, they gradually internalise and do to themselves. Thus, children who have been constantly criticised gradually become convinced that they are inadequate and so criticise themselves.

The child can accommodate widely different versions or views of the self. One part of the self, what has been called the 'good me', grows out of experiences of being praised, loved, responded to. The more the child attracts such affirmation, the more expansive and robust the 'good me' and the higher the self-esteem. The 'bad me', on the other hand, is that part of the child's self that has attracted criticism, disapproval and punishment. If few aspects of the child's appearance, impulses or behaviour are free of such criticism, the 'bad me' can predominate in the child's sense of self. Less commonly, there may be substantial parts of its self that are so threatening to the child that they are pushed out of consciousness altogether and become the 'not me'. This buried or rejected part of the self is normally experienced only in nightmares, irrational dreads and anxieties.

It is the part of self that can partially emerge at periods of great psychological crisis, such as the break-up of a marriage, when otherwise normal adults suddenly find themselves full of murderous feelings or panic about being psychologically annihilated. Everybody has an unconscious, or 'not me' part of self, of course, but this is normally contained within a strong ego. For children who have experienced severe parental rejection or abuse, a large part of themselves becomes too threatening or painful to be acknowledged and instead forms a destructive potential at the very centre of self.

Towards the end of middle childhood, children also develop

an ideal self — an image of the kind of person they would like to be. The ideal self serves a vital psychological function as children actively try to shape their behaviour towards this ideal. It helps them to work hard in school, make good resolutions, and generally to stake out the territory in which the self will be invested. Self-esteem comes to be identified with competence in certain things, for example, being clever, being nice, being good at sports. Other activities that the child does not like, or feels he or she cannot master, are defined as 'off-limits' or irrelevant to self-esteem. Clearly, self-esteem is shaky if too many arenas to demonstrate achievement or too many opportunities for success are defined as 'off-limits'.

What kind of parents produce children with high self-esteem? Studies show them to be accepting, affectionate and involved. They take a real interest in their children's affairs and know their children's friends. They are concerned about their children's day-to-day problems and, most importantly, consider these problems to be legitimate. They believe it is important for children to meet high standards and so they instil in their children the sense that they can meet these standards. Perhaps surprisingly, they tend to be somewhat strict; they enforce rules and exercise a fairly high level of control. They are firm and decisive in telling the child what he or she might or might not do and, most important, discuss with their children why certain forms of behaviour are good or bad. Yet, they use relatively little physical punishment or withdrawal of love. They allow their children to express their own opinions and to have their own way some of the time. They do not discourage their children from questioning the parents' point of view and they allow them to participate in making family plans.

Why is firm control so important? Because, in giving the child a clear idea of the right way to behave, they are helping the child to understand how to please them and minimising the child's anxiety as to how they will react. They are thus creating a predictable, ordered environment in which it is easier for the child to feel in control. Although parental restrictions may irritate the child on occasion, they are often seen as proof that their parents care. The parent saying 'Do whatever you like, just don't bother me' is giving the message that the child is not worthy of concern.

But just as setting limits teaches children to acknowledge forces outside themselves, they must also themselves be given the experience of power and control. That is why parents must be responsive to their children. The successful child-rearing formula for self-esteem, then, is to allow the child a sense of control in the context of a firm, orderly and decisive parenting style. In such a partnership, the parent does not feel manipulated, and the child will rarely read irritation and resentment in the parent's eyes. Instead, the child strives to be good — seeking and finding the powerful message of approval.

Treat Your Children Well

Even the wisest, most scrupulously fair parent is put in the children's dock once a day. Children have a highly developed sense of justice and fair play, a sixth sense capable of detecting the slightest parental favouritism. Yet, despite the efforts of parents and children to declare the family a republic of equality and fraternity, all the children may not be equally cherished. A certain child delights you, makes you proud, is easy, fits into the family way of doing things. Another child constantly gets on your nerves, causes trouble, is hard to handle, is different from the rest of the family.

Some children of course are difficult. There is now considerable evidence that children are born with very different temperaments and that temperament can act to protect a child or put them at risk in the family. Some parents have great trouble accepting that no two children are the same. They feel disappointed and frustrated by a temperamentally difficult child and see the child's difficulties in fitting in with them as somehow accusatory, as if the child were saying to them: 'If you were a good parent, I would not act like this.'

This 'accusation' from the child may fill parents — particularly those with low self-esteem — with such feelings of helpless rage or frustration that they turn the accusation back on the child. They begin to describe the child as unlovable, impossibly alien to them and to their way of doing things. In time, the child may come to be blamed for other problems in the family. Sometimes this scapegoating is very open and shocking. The child may be singled out for special punishment or be placed psychologically outside the family. The child may be repeatedly told, 'I don't know where we got you at all; there's something about you that makes me think you never belonged to me at all.'

At other times the scapegoating may be more subtle or may

surface only when the parent is under particular stress. Then, it is as if the scapegoated child becomes the butt of everybody's frustration, attracting criticism and irritability like a spire attracts lightning. Children who are rejected or who are constantly compared badly to their siblings begin to act with conviction the part of bad boy or bad girl. The child may try to get attention or avoid punishment by becoming the family clown, the rebel, the one who sneaks on the others. The parent's original view of the child as inadequate, hard to love or a problem is reinforced by the child's self-destructive striving to be accepted, loved and treated fairly.

Sometimes a child is singled out for special treatment — positive and negative — because he or she reminds the parent of a significant person in the parent's own life. For a parent who harbours strong unresolved feelings about that particular person from their childhood, this resemblance can be unnerving. The parent begins an anxious search for other similarities. 'Will my son, who is so like my brother, turn out to be a bully like him? Will my daughter, who looks like my mother, also reject me?'

The physical resemblance may act like a magnetic field, attracting all the associations, feelings and energy of the old relationship. Thus, the child can be cherished, favoured, held up as the legitimate psychological heir to all that was good in the parent's own family; or the child can become the wretched receptacle of all the anger, rivalry, resentment and disappointment that characterised the parent's relationship with some key figure from the past.

Being the family favourite can, of course, confer significant psychological advantages on a child. Such a child, after all, has a hotline to the parent's heart. But it can also significantly affect how that child relates to siblings. Children are naturally in competition with each other, but not exclusively so. They also are intensely attached to one another. Playing favourites can rob a child of his or her brothers and sisters. For a child who is favoured, the envy, jealousy and bitterness engendered in the other children can poison relationships. The favoured child is distanced from the others by the special rights and privileges he or she is accorded by the parents. Such a child may become the other children's intermediary with the parents, rather like a school prefect, bargaining on their behalf or bossing them about.

Such power is irresistible to children and can give them a lifelong appetite for dominance in relationships. But, as they get older, favoured children may want to be closer to their brothers and sisters. Their developing sense of what is right and wrong may make them uncomfortable with their privileged position within the family. In adolescence, they may try to restore balance to family relationships by forming alliances with their siblings against their parents. They may consciously or unconsciously go against their parents' expectations for them personally, abdicating their role as family heir.

Most parents intuitively know that it is wrong to relate to a child on the basis of old associations. Although their real feelings for the child may be indeed different, they operate an intricate system of checks and balances so that the child is not treated any differently — better or worse — than the other children. But sometimes, in an attempt to cover up their real feelings, parents may go to the opposite extreme, lavishing attention on or overprotecting the very child for whom their feelings are most in doubt.

Children usually detect their parents' underlying feelings, particularly where those feelings are negative. They will quickly pick up signs of emotional reserve or watchfulness on the part of the parents. Often such children become emotionally withdrawn themselves, unconsciously recognising that it is dangerous to enquire too deeply into the true feelings of others.

But even if a child has some inkling of the parents' difficulty in accepting them, the very fact that the parents desire so intensely to reach out means that strong bonds develop. There is an earned, working quality to the parent-child relationship that makes it unusually vital and responsive. Parents may find that, even if their feelings are initially beyond their control, their behaviour is not. And, of course, when behaviour changes, feelings often change too. By healing fraught relations with a child, parents often succeed in healing some of their own wounds too. They themselves grow up in the process of trying to be good parents.

'Don't Touch Me'

All parents routinely touch their children while caring for them. But the way in which that touching is done, and what is communicated by it, makes a great difference to the child's psychological development.

Even when the child is at a distance, some parents manage to communicate that they would like to be touched, while others communicate aloofness and a lack of approachability. This 'touch accessibility' is critical to a child when he wants to be held and comforted. It is also the factor which very often differentiates between mothers who are going to have securely or insecurely attached babies.

The key distinction is between touch simply as 'handling or manipulation' — a means to an end — and touch as 'laying hands on' or 'reaching out and communicating' — an end in itself. It is this latter, more complex sense of touch that we all intuitively recognise when we talk about 'being touched by your kindness' or 'feeling for you', almost as if there was an energy field flowing between people.

But surely the desire to touch and be touched by your own infant must be instinctive? Not for everybody, it seems. The eminent American psychologist, Mary Main, discovered that some mothers have an aversion to physical contact with their young children, though they themselves may be unaware of this. This was discovered in the course of an American observational study of the attachment of twelve-month-old babies to their mothers. Most of the babies were found to be securely attached, but several patterns of insecure attachment were also identified. These insecure attachment patterns are now known to be related to a wide range of emotional and behavioural problems at later stages of the child's development.

Children who showed one particular pattern of insecure attachment were found to have mothers who cared for them in a stiff, emotionless way. This did not mean that the mothers did not hold the children. Rather, it was the manner in which they held the children that was distinctive.

Observations at home had revealed that this group of mothers had a physical aversion to touching as early as the first three months of the child's life, although observers at this point were not aware that it was these particular mother-infant pairs who would later develop problems with attachment. The mothers often said that their babies had not been cuddly. Yet the observers could find no evidence of this.

The mothers exhibited a constellation of behaviours which indicated, in more or less obvious ways, their reluctance to have contact with their babies. Not every mother in the group consistently reacted in exactly the same way, but here are some of the signs most frequently reported by the observers:

• When seated, the mother would keep her knees up or hold herself in such a position that the infant could not reach her lap. She might arch back or away as the infant approached, sometimes even wincing or flinching when the child moved into closer contact.

• She might fold her arms across her stomach, as though to prevent the child from touching her, especially when the infant was sitting on her lap or trying to sit on it. She was prepared to remain in, or even move into, an uncomfortable position, rather than relax into a better position which would bring her into contact with the infant. For example, the mother, while holding the infant, might move her neck and head back at an awkward angle in order to reduce or avoid contact. In another situation, she might keep her shoulders well back, rather than curved towards the infant in the attentive, receptive posture adopted by other mothers.

• The mother would often keep the middle of her body — chest, stomach and lap — angled away from the infant.

• She would fail to shift posture in order to 'follow' the infant's movements. Normally, mothers will constantly, and almost unconsciously, reposition their own bodies to accommodate a jiggling baby.

• A mother in this group also tended to keep her head at a different level from that of the infant, making no effort to align the baby's head with hers in order to allow eye contact.

Perhaps the best way to understand the situation from the mother's point of view is to think of the kind of tense posture we adopt when trying to avoid contact with somebody sitting too near us on a bus or train. From the young child's point of view, of course, the situation is much more serious than simple physical discomfort: the mother's signals tend to deeply confuse the child. Despite the baby's longing for touch, the mother is suggesting by her behaviour that she believes the baby does not want contact, that there is no occasion for contact, or that she might not like contact even if the baby wanted it.

The mothers often said to the baby things such as: 'You know I hate to have you crawling all over me', or 'Don't touch me'. They habitually stiffened while holding the baby, tended to push him away, or angrily shouted at him when he was making a bid for contact. These were not the occasional episodes of irritation to which the most saintly or receptive mothers are prey. Rather, the aversion to physical touch was a stable characteristic.

The rebuffing can be more indirect, with the mother, for example, constantly offering the child a toy or a biscuit, instead of responding to his bid to be held. Again, she may avoid looking at the child, or returning his gaze, in case it should lead to contact.

The child's potential approach movements are thus discouraged. He feels rejected in the original sense of that word 'turning back or away'.

The whole function of an attachment figure, of course, is to be a safe haven when a baby is distressed or afraid, and the ultimate form of security is physical contact. What happens, then, when the primary attachment figure, usually the mother, is herself the source of alarm? If the baby is lucky, he will be able to turn to another attachment figure, a loving father or a granny perhaps. If such a person is not available, the baby simply has to give up on the possibility of attachment to anybody. Without relief, the infant soon takes on the mother's pattern.

By twelve months of age, the insecurely attached babies of the 'avoidant' mothers tended to avoid touch themselves. When separated briefly from their mothers in a laboratory situation, they showed no obvious distress. In addition, they ignored the mother when she returned — unlike the securely attached children, who immediately sought contact. If the avoidant mother picked up the child, he would often indicate that he wanted to be put down. He would not do this in an obvious way by struggling, but in an indirect way — by bending towards the floor or by pointing towards an object, as if to distract the mother's attention. Yet these children only *appeared* to be indifferent. Physiological measures showed that they were in fact highly anxious.

Perhaps the saddest aspect of this is that young mothers who are averse to touching their children have usually been physically rejected by their own mothers. They do not choose to repeat history out of some wilful indifference. Rather, the child's distress and need for comfort unconsciously arouse painful memories of the mothers' own misery. In an attempt to exclude these unhappy memories, they ignore the child's search for physical closeness.

It scarcely needs to be said that it would be both pointless and unfair to blame the mothers themselves. They often have an unrealistic and idealised view of the past, tending to say things like 'I had a perfect childhood' or 'My mother was a great person'. At the same time, they have little detailed recollection of childhood, or else recount anecdotes that are in direct contradiction to the idealised picture. For example, they may recall being ridiculed, neglected, or never having been held. But they are unable to integrate these negative features into the story of their early life.

The very complexity of touch behaviour suggests how maternal rejection, when it is expressed in this way, is more often felt than understood. The mother who rejects at a non-verbal level may be simultaneously taking good functional care of the child and, at a rational, conscious level, may have the highest possible ideals as a parent. She may even remind the child from time to time of what a good and self-sacrificing mother she is. It is hardly surprising that the child in such a case has confusing and contradictory memories.

We are only now beginning to appreciate how a person's developing sense of self is rooted in body awareness; how our adult self-esteem is connected to the manner in which we were touched as infants. And how subtle are the ways in which we first come to know that we are worth loving.

The Toddler in the Teen

The American psychologist Joseph Tobin begins his course on adolescence by asking his class: 'Imagine that tomorrow you wake up and discover that your sex drive has increased ten-fold. Think about what effects that would have on you — on your body-image, concentration, appetite, energy levels, on your ability to enjoy old and new pleasures, on every aspect of your personal relationships. Imagine how all those changes would affect your sense of yourself and then you will have some inkling of what the experience of puberty is like for adolescents.'

It is a good way to start thinking about adolescence, which is best understood as the sum total of all the attempts the young person has to make to adjust to the novel condition of puberty, to all the internal and external demands that now confront him or her. At no other stage in life, bar early infancy, is physical growth so rapid and dramatic. But unlike infancy, the adolescent is now the fascinated, bewildered and at times appalled observer of these dramatic changes.

Puberty typically begins sometime between the age of nine and fourteen. Somewhere inside the child's body a mighty and mysterious force is bringing childhood to an end and is starting the process that will end with an adult, sexually mature body. Gradually, it seeps into every aspect of the self. It creates new urges, new ways to feel close to others, new needs to be alone. These new urges come into conflict with the old ways of doing things; there is a feeling of disequilibrium, at times, of the centre not holding.

Parallel to the biological changes is the intellectual maturation. For the first time, the adolescent has the capacity to think in terms of possibility rather than merely concrete reality. In contrast to childhood, when thinking and problem-solving tend to be practical and grounded in reality, adolescent thinking subordinates reality to possibility. Adolescents find that they can speculate, hypothesise, fantasise, build theories about love, life, morality and themselves — their past, present and future.

As the elemental force of puberty changes the young person's body, body image and very sense of self, a question arises that never arose in childhood: 'Who am I?' That search for identity becomes the primary task and crisis of adolescence. Jung believed that the psychological struggle throughout the lifespan is to become more and more yourself, to continually discover and sculpt your own sense of individual uniqueness. In adolescence, according to psychoanalyst Peter Blos, a second step in becoming your own person occurs, the first one having happened towards the end of the second year of life, when the child experiences the fateful distinction between the 'self' and the 'non-self'. A similar, yet far more complex, step in individuation happens during the adolescent years and leads to a sense of identity that is the hallmark of adulthood.

It is a complex process. The young person has to consciously fashion a sense of individual uniqueness and at the same time find a place that is satisfying, first in the peer group and then in society. But there is also an unconscious striving to maintain a sense of continuity with the past. In the process of adolescents 'finding themselves', the significant emotional needs and conflicts of childhood are re-evaluated, worked over and over, until they yield the new solutions necessary to go forward into the next stage and confront its challenges. It is a process that will be repeated at all the major transition points in adult life: marriage, becoming a parent, middle age, retirement, facing death. Thus adolescence has been called the second edition of childhood, and mid-life 'middlescence', the second edition of adolescence. It is worth recalling the first step in individuation that occurred in the second year of life to see just how similar the dynamic is to what happens in adolescence. Most parents will remember the transformation of their malleable baby into the strong-willed and stubborn toddler. The transformation of the malleable schoolchild into the headstrong and rebellious teenager bears striking parallels.

The toddler, at the end of his or her first year, discovers that the parent is a separate person. Up until then, the infant does not know where his or her body ends and the mother's begins. This new experience of separateness brings ambivalent feelings. On the positive side, it brings a sense of control and competence; the toddler is developing new skills almost daily and he/she cannot wait to try them out. On the negative side, this awareness of being separate brings with it feelings of loneliness and confusion. Gone is the blissful security of childhood, when the parent could fulfil nearly all the child's needs. Despite the new-found competence and skills, the toddler discovers that the world can be a frustrating place.

The developmental task that confronts toddlers is to negotiate the appropriate distance between themselves and parents. If there is too much closeness, toddlers will never grow up. If there is too little, toddlers flounder. Mostly, they will teeter between the pleasure of autonomy and the pain of loss. One day they want to be grown-ups; the next, to be babied. These polarities of progress-regression, activity-passivity, independence-dependency account for the characteristic ambivalence of the 'terrible twos'. In adolescence, all these ambivalences are again evoked. No matter how frustrating, frightening and lonely it is for toddlers to experience that they are separate persons, that is what has to be done to achieve a sense of self. Toddlers do it in a characteristic way, by trial and error, by experimentation, by testing the self, by going to excess, by opposition. Parents will recall the emotional highs and lows of family life in the wake of toddler 'experiments', frenetic physical activities and discovery of the word 'no'. That is the only way young children can learn how the world works and the limits of what they can do.

Toddlers first learn to stake out their territory and learn about 'me' and 'mine' by using the word 'no'. This is the first step away from the parents. Toddlers still do not know enough about themselves to make a positive choice. 'Yes' is still bound up with the parent as part of the self, the provider. 'No' is finding out about self.

In adolescence, these ways of learning come again to the fore. Before adolescents can answer the question 'Who am I?' they pass through stages of intense self-consciousness, experimentation and negativity. Resistance is often manifested in a negativity that parents find irrational and hurtful. Yet this negativity is serving two important developmental purposes. The adolescent does not yet know who he or she is, but a first step is knowing what he or she is not. This negativity, expressed as rejection of values or role-models that parents approve of, is a way of saying 'this is not me', the first step in achieving a sense of oneself as an individual. It also serves as a defence against the unconscious pull of regression, the temptation to remain a child.

Just as the toddler had to give up the feeling of omnipotence, when the all-powerful parent was perceived as part of the self, the adolescent has to give up the gratifying ties and grandiose dreams of childhood and gradually learn to shape an independent life. The process of individuation necessarily involves a constant reworking of the dynamic of psychological separation and attachment: to what extent am I autonomous and alone? to what extent am I connected to others?

Similarly, in mid-life, the prize of a more authentic sense of self can be bought only by an acceptance that many of the dreams of early adulthood will not now be achieved, and by realising, in a new and urgent way, that there is a only a finite amount of time left to make hard decisions and choices, to leave a mark. That sense of urgency and fear in mid-life, the feeling that 'it's now or never', has its echo in the feelings adolescents have as they stand, anxious and expectant, on the verge of adulthood. They too have to make hard decisions and choices. They too feel that for them 'it's now or never'; they have to become somebody, to get a foothold in life, or they may be left behind forever. How they negotiate this second step in individuation will depend in part on how the first step was experienced in their second year of life and will shape in turn how mid-life will be managed.

Changing Body, Changing Self

The biological event of puberty sets in train a series of physical, cognitive and emotional changes that in ten years will transform a child into an adult. Trying to adapt to those changes is the stuff of adolescence. Puberty typically begins sometime between the ages of nine and fourteen. The first signs of this momentous event — increased concentrations of male and female hormones in the body — are invisible. It takes about a year before the results of these hormonal changes — the initial enlargement of the breasts in girls and the testes in boys — become visible to the young person. It takes about another year before the first sign of puberty — the growth spurt — is observable to others.

During the year of greatest growth, a girl can gain as much as twenty pounds and three inches, and a boy up to twenty-six pounds and four inches. Yet friends of the same age may not grow much at all during that same year. Worse, the growth spurt does not happen in every part of the body simultaneously. In most cases, adolescents' hands and feet lengthen before their arms and legs do, and their trunk is the last part to grow. Their noses, lips and ears usually grow before their head reaches adult size and shape and, if all that wasn't enough, the two halves of the body do not always grow at the same rate. One foot, breast or ear can temporarily outgrow the other. It is hardly surprising then that, at the beginning of adolescence, young people spend long periods closeted in the bathroom anxiously examining themselves in the mirror.

Despite the extraordinary individual variability, the changes of puberty occur in predictable sequence and tempo. For girls, the hormonal changes will produce, usually in sequence and at these average ages, the beginning of breast development (age 10), first pubic hair (age 11), the growth spurt (age 12), peak muscle and organ growth, including widening of hips (age 12),

21

first menstrual period (age 12), first ovulation (age 13), full breast growth (age 16). For boys, the hormonal changes will produce, usually in sequence and at these average ages, the growth of the testes and scrotum (age 11), first pubic hair (age 12), growth of the penis (age 12), first ejaculation (age 13), height spurt (age 14), peak muscle and organ growth, including widening of shoulders (age 14), deepening of the voice (age 15), first facial hair (age 16).

Adolescents not only have to cope with a changing body, but also with a body that almost inevitably does not live up to their exacting standards. Few adolescents are satisfied with their looks. For example, one study showed that nearly 50 per cent of adolescent boys wanted to be taller and almost the same proportion of girls wished to be thinner. Boys worry about the size of their penis and girls worry about the size of their breasts — as well as the shape of their buttocks, legs, knees and feet. In one experiment, adolescents and adults were blindfolded and asked to identify an object — an upside-down mask of their own face — by touch. The young teenagers were the quickest to do so. Apparently their intense preoccupation with every nook and cranny of their faces compensated for the fact that theirs were the faces that were changing the fastest and therefore were the hardest to recognise.

The adolescents who have the most difficulty adjusting to the changes in their body are those who mature earlier or later than their peers. Girls usually mature before boys, so it is not surprising that the girls who mature early and the boys who mature late, because they represent the two extremes with regard to the timing of puberty, are most vulnerable. Early maturing girls in fifth or sixth class in primary school may have no friend with whom to share their new-found interest in boys or their new anxieties about their bodies. They may be subjected to teasing by boys about their breasts and big feet. If they start to date boys, they may attract unwelcome, intrusive attention from their parents, and criticism from their friends, who feel neglected and themselves are uncertain and worried about what exactly 'getting off' with boys means. However, if girls who mature early can survive the stresses of the first few years of adolescence, they can convert their biological advantage into increased status and popularity with their peers, who now look to them for advice about bodies, bras and kissing boys.

Late-maturing boys face another set of problems that are potentially more serious. Unlike girls, early maturation confers status on boys, giving them a boisterous self-assurance and a sense of superiority over their less mature peers. As a consequence, the late maturing boy is more likely to be consigned to the end of the male hierarchy in the class. The resulting stress is reflected in the fact that they are less relaxed and poised than their early-maturing friends, more agitated and restless. Perhaps as compensation, they often adopt the role of class troublemaker, 'suck', 'swot' or clown. They are also more likely to be playful, creative and flexible, but these qualities earn them little credit with other teenage boys.

Some studies have shown that, even in adulthood, those who had matured late tend to be less controlled, less dominant and less likely to hold leadership positions in their work or social lives and some still suffered from feelings of inferiority. However, on the positive side, they were also more likely to be humorous, perceptive and egalitarian in their adult relationships. Despite the problems, some early-maturing boys cope very well, particularly if they are encouraged by family and school to develop their academic and creative abilities and — this is important — their sense of humour.

As well as the physical development of adolescence, there is psychological development. Each young person makes the journey to adulthood in his or her own way. This fact cannot be stressed too much. However, despite the individual variability, there remains an orderly sequence of psychological development that happens in more or less distinct phases: pre-adolescence, early, middle, late adolescence and post-adolescence. These phases correspond very roughly to ages 10 – 11, 12 – 13, 14 –15, 16 – 17, 18 – 19, but of course much depends on the individual's temperament, family and social context, and the timing of puberty itself.

The adolescent can rush through these various phases or can get stuck for a long time in one, but eventually he or she will have to confront the psychological tasks embedded in each of the phases. The ultimate goal of adolescence is to achieve a sense of identity, a stable sense of self. The novel event of puberty and all the changes it provokes are eventually knitted into the older experience and personality of childhood. Out of the range of memories, values and choices available, the adolescent rejects some, accepts others and thus gradually begins to shape an authentic sense of self.

For some young people, this search for identity is precarious. Too much unfinished business from childhood, family pressures or low self-esteem can force a young person into premature identity formation, what the psychoanalyst Erik Erikson called 'foreclosure'. Such young people are characterised by a tendency to be defensive and to repress anxiety. They are loving and respectful towards parents and tend to have impulsive, dependent and rather stereotyped relations with others. They accept the role assigned to them by their parents and uncritically conform to family pressures and values, without ever exploring alternatives.

Sometimes it is clear that the young person is consciously try-ing to please parents. At other times, apparently free choices ('It's what I really want to do myself') mask an unconscious feeling of parental pressure. A young person may feel so fundamentally insecure with their parents, that every decision and choice will be shaped unconsciously by the desire to get the love, acceptance and affirmation they crave from them. It may be halfway through a college degree, or even in middle age, that the person comes to understand that they have allowed their one and only life to be shaped by somebody else's agenda.

Other young people are clear that they either do not want or cannot achieve what parents and society expect of them, but they cannot articulate an alternative. They then take on a negative identity — the opposite of what is expected of them. The child of devoutly religious parents, for example, may give up all observ-ance or even join a cult. The child of academically high-achieving parents may drop out of school to join a rock group. Of course, many adolescents go through such phases. However, taking on a negative identity permanently is quite different. Then, the forward movement of adolescence is stalled and the energies of the young person are just as surely trapped by a preoccupation with parents as if the adolescent was fully conforming to them.

Other adolescents cannot seem to get going at all. Some of or all the tasks of adolescence — completing school, making friends, planning for the future — are too much for them. They have no clear sense of themselves, no commitment to any goals or values in which to anchor themselves. They drift, experiencing their identity as diffuse, outside of their grasp. These young people tend to be withdrawn and isolated, often sleeping a lot, as a way of avoiding interaction.

Another pattern is to declare a moratorium. Some adolescents explore alternative identities, without having to settle on any one for the time being. They consciously try to distance themselves from their family, but, unlike the withdrawn adolescent, they are doing so with a strong purpose. They may become intensely interested in artistic or environmental pursuits, working in the Third World or travelling. They have high self-esteem and tend to be reflective and self-directed, although they may be experiencing a lot of anxiety.

The adolescents who most easily achieve a strong sense of identity are found to be reflective and self-directed, with a loving and caring attitude towards parents and close relationships with others. However, research shows that many adolescents go through a period of foreclosure or diffusion and then a moratorium before they finally achieve a sense of identity. The process can take ten years or more. Flawed or compromise solutions to identity may remain relatively stable throughout young adulthood and may then resurface in mid-life in feelings of anger, loss or despair, in the painful realisation that your life has been stolen from you, that your talents were wasted, that you never got going.

The Golden Period of Childhood

Successful adolescence is rooted in the period of childhood that immediately precedes it, what psychoanalysts call the latency period, which corresponds roughly with the primary school years. This is the time when, psychologically, two important things are happening. First, the structure of the ego is being built. The ego can be understood as the executive part of the personality, the part that helps us to keep in touch with reality, make judgments, resist impulses, achieve an inner sense of control, learn to understand and empathise with others. Second, the child's self-esteem is gradually becoming anchored in achievements and mastery which earn praise and affirmation from parents, teachers and friends. Thus, the child is not as wholly dependent on the unconditional responsiveness of parents (although that always remains vital) but is in more control of what makes him or her feel secure and happy.

This is the golden period of childhood. Aware of their own immaturity, children have given up the passionate longings, rivalries and disappointments that characterised relationships with parents in early childhood and, instead, have identified with the parents, particularly with the same-sex parent. Since they cannot have the opposite-sex parent all to themselves, they resolve instead to become like the same-sex parent, to borrow their strength, until they have become mature enough to have an exclusive, adult love of their own. In the eyes of the child, the parent of the school years is a colossus: the source of wisdom, the refuge in stress, the provider of dreams, the key to the future.

During this period of stability, the internal personality development and the external achievements in the world together make the child ready for the dramatic changes of puberty. In this way, when the new sexual drive of puberty surges within, the child is able to divert that potentially chaotic energy into a well-organised personality structure and a stable set of relationships, interests and achievements, rather than experience it solely as an increase in sexual and aggressive tension. This is important because during pre-adolescence, in the period just before the appearance of the secondary sex characteristics (male/female body shape, breasts, pubic hair), the rise in male and female hormones is such that it can make almost anything sexually stimulating. Erections, for example, can be provoked by anger, fear, general excitement, stress. For the child who is not securely anchored inside and outside, this barely understood new energy can be experienced as threatening, disorganising, destabilising.

Unconscious preoccupation with the sex organs — what they can do, are they OK? can they be injured? — may be reflected in play during this phase. For example, many of the games and toys that boys of this age enjoy are concerned with things that can go up and down and fire missiles (for example, 'action' or 'power' figures; cars or trucks that can 'transform' themselves into powerful missiles). Similarly, girls' unconscious sexual preoccupation with internal spaces that can be opened or closed, blocked or intruded on is reflected in the toys they enjoy (dolls' houses, hopscotch).

The increase in drive also reawakens the preoccupations of infancy and early childhood — concerns with bodily functions and bodily integrity. There is an increase in oral greediness, a new pleasure in 'dirty' language, a fascination with odours. Jokes about bottoms, lavatories and where babies come from are all revived from early childhood. The mere mention of a word with any sexual connotation can send groups of children of this age into excited laughing that can easily get out of control. The parent begins to notice that their heretofore accommodating child is becoming more difficult to reach and to control.

This new surge of sexual interest and the accompanying impulses make children of this age feel unconsciously anxious and guilty. This is the time when they may develop minor compulsive habits, obsessional fears, phobias and nervous tics. For example, they may start to bite their nails, stutter, twist their mouths to the side, fiddle compulsively with their hair. These habits help them to regulate the tension they feel inside.

The primitive fears of infancy are also revived. For example, in early childhood, to achieve the first step in a masculine identity, to become 'a big boy', the boy had to renounce and repress his identification with his mother, his infantile longings for passivity, his unconscious wish to stay a baby and even have a baby. In order to identify with his father, to avoid defeat by the stronger male, he also had to renounce his rivalry with him. This triangular conflict — the crucible of sexual identity — is what Freud called the 'Oedipus complex'. But for the young child, this process of renunciation and repression takes a long time to complete. His masculinity is easily threatened by longings from within that may surface, especially when he is distressed or experiences external defeat by another male. This feeling of threat gets focused on the penis, the badge of masculinity. This is what Freud termed 'castration anxiety'.

As the boy develops throughout the school years, he becomes better able to repress that castration anxiety. Faced at the beginning of puberty with the resurgence of old infantile desires and fears and the challenge of achieving a more adult masculinity, castration anxiety is again revived. Unconsciously he tries to protect himself from any threat to his masculinity. This is the stage when boys become very hostile to girls and will go to any lengths to avoid them. To assert their masculinity, they typically belittle and tease girls, while at the same time covertly trying to impress them by boasting and showing off. In games of football in the school yard, when they suspect that the girls are looking, boys throw themselves to the ground in heroic tackles.

A boy at this stage may also express highly aggressive impulses towards the mother's body — as a defence against his re-awakened infantile desire to be nurtured by her or his infantile fear that she may devour him. Thus, the typical conflict for the pre-adolescent boy is fear and envy of the female. By banding together defensively with other boys, by striving for glory and achievement, the boy is affirming again and again 'I'm glad I'm a boy'. The more powerfully the mother figures in his psyche, the bigger the threat, but also the greater the achievement when he succeeds in resolving his status with her. Again and again he is affirming 'Look at me. I'm a boy and I'm the best'. In that way the boy takes another step towards resolving his bisexual identity and is ready for the next stage of adolescence.

For girls, the first step in achieving a sexual identity has also taken place in the triangular oedipal relationship. But, although she has to renounce her striving to be like and possess her father, she does not have to make a psychic break from her primary attachment and identification with her mother, like the boy does. Moreover, her renunciation of her wish to be like her father (what Freud called 'penis envy') never has to be done as forcefully as the boy has to renounce his wish to be like his mother. There are strong social taboos against 'girlish' or 'sissy' boys, but quite a lot of tolerance for tomboys. As a consequence, the girl can wait until adolescence to come to terms with her bisexuality and her remaining deep attachment to her mother.

Thus, in pre-adolescence, tomboyish behaviour and rivalry with boys is very marked. This is the time when girls often become besotted by horses and horseriding. Psychoanalyst Peter Blos, who analysed the dreams of pre-adolescent girls, believed that the horse represents the girl's identification with her father. The horse is both a powerful, thrusting phallus, her 'masculine', striving side, and the object of devoted, loving daughterly care.

A girl at this stage tends to become competitive with boys, who are haughtily dismissed as 'nerds', and she can develop a formidable skill in verbal put-downs. Because of her continuing attachment to her mother, the pre-adolescent girl defends herself against the regressive pull of staying a child by a forceful and decisive turn towards the opposite sex. Already more sexually mature than her male counterparts, she takes the initiative in these early encounters with boys. Her struggle to find a good balance between autonomy and attachment in her relationship with her mother may result in many conflicts between them at this stage. More generally, it is in the matrix of relationships with family, friends and boyfriends that the girl will struggle to achieve her identity as a young woman. Again and again she is affirming 'You are important to me. I want to be close but I also want to be different, acknowledged as "me".'

At the end of this phase, before the advent of adolescence proper, important psychological progress has been made.

Despite the revival of infantile fears, pre-adolescent children have resisted the temptation to regress; they have begun to liberate themselves from the dependency and control of childhood; they have taken another step towards a secure sexual identity. They are now poised to face the challenges of adolescence.

Peers, Tears and Early Adolescence

Just as the biological goal at the end of adolescence is an adult, sexually mature body, the psychological goal is the achievement of identity and character. Thus, a profound reorganisation of the young person's emotional life must take place. At the beginning of adolescence, the child's passive need to be loved, to be given to, to be 'done to', gradually gives rise to new active needs: to love, to give, 'to do' to another. The need to be active, in control, rather than to be passive and controlled, assumes a new urgency. This polarity of activity-passivity becomes a crucial issue in adolescence and is inextricably linked to the development of masculinity and femininity.

This change from a more passive to a more active role is not straightforward. Adolescents remain ambivalent about giving up the role of dependent child. Thus, one day they want to be grown-up, the next to be babied. All extremes of being passive and active may be tried and they may swing unpredictably between the two. Thus, young adolescents may demand to be allowed into town alone, yet become outraged if the parent will not act as a chauffeur. One day there is intense physical activity, wildly overambitious plans and an apparent inability to make any decision without consulting friends on the phone; the next day, inertia, despondency and moody withdrawal.

The stronger the unconscious pull to stay dependent, the stronger the psychological defence against it. This often takes the form of rebellious behaviour and is more likely to happen if the adolescent was either too indulged and overprotected or was deprived as a child. Either of those extremes tends to produce very strong dependency needs in children which can create difficulties in adolescence. That is why parents are frequently bewildered by what they see as the incomprehensible transformation of 'the child who was given everything' or the child they hardly noticed into a sullen and hostile teenager.

Dependency and attachment are key concepts in adolescence. For the young person, at the beginning of adolescence, the parent is the primary attachment figure, the person to whom they will turn for comfort and security, especially when distressed, the person who serves as their secure base. Gradually that primary attachment will be transferred to the intimate partner of adulthood. Friends will play an important part in that crucial transition.

First, the childlike identification with parents, established in early childhood, is slowly dismantled. It was that intense wish to become like the parent that enabled the child to first try to please parents by submitting to their control and eventually to internalise parental values. In other words, identification allowed the development of conscience. As the young person begins to separate psychologically from his or her parents and identifies less with them, conscience also weakens in a temporary way, often reflected in lessened self-control and acting-out behaviour (temper-tantrums, minor anti-social acts, illicit drinking and smoking).

This psychological separation from parents often leaves the adolescent feeling empty and confused. However, while the young person has not yet formed a stable set of values and standards to replace the parental standards of childhood, something else is happening to fill the gap. Friends and peers assume a new importance. The pressure to conform to the peer group rises dramatically in early adolescence, reaching a peak at about age fourteen. Parents naturally worry about the negative influence of such peer pressure. However, there is evidence that peers can and do play a positive role, functioning as a self-help group to allow adolescents to explore new identities, cope with self-doubts, and compensate for any lack of intimacy with parents. A large mixed-group circle has the additional benefit of allowing the young person to think about, talk about and associate with the opposite sex without the intensity experienced in 'going out' with one person. Not only is teenage sex more unlikely in that scenario, but the most crucial single predictor of an adolescent's future achievement and psychological well-being is the ability to get along well with friends.

For the adolescent, the process of finding their own identity and set of values does not require, and rarely ends, with a complete rejection of their parents' values. Very often, they end up with the same values and goals, particularly with regard to education, career, religion and politics. But, through a process of questioning and experimenting, they must make those goals and values their own, put their own mark on them. Just like the mid-life transition, the person may emerge at the end of the adolescent transition with what looks like the same life and the same values, but psychologically they are different — they have found a new angle, have committed themselves to the old goals in a new way.

For the adolescent, the critical element of this process is forming some idea about his or her ideal self. Thinking about and trying to achieve this ideal absorbs much of the adolescent's free-floating energy. It also serves as an internal standard, allowing the young person to reject behaviour or relationships that are perceived to be incompatible with that ideal ('This is not the kind of person I want to be'). Thus, parents often wryly note that while their standards and strictures are frequently derided, resisted or 'forgotten' by their adolescent children, the self-imposed standards about being 'cool' or avoiding being 'sad' are adhered to with almost puritanical zeal. Nothing is too much work or trouble for a teenager if it can be linked to their self-ideal.

An external sign of the newly developing ideal self may be the adolescent's search for a special friend. This friend will not be the same as the friends of childhood, but rather will have some characteristic that the young person admires intensely and would like to have for him- or herself. The special friend, according to Freud, acts as 'a substitute for the lost narcissism of his childhood in which he was his own ideal'.

For both sexes, but particularly for girls, these special friendships take the form of a 'crush', a heady mixture of idealisation and erotic attachment. One man, remembering his 'crush' on a senior boy at school, described the experience thus: 'I remember following him around. I couldn't take my eyes off him. I thought he was just perfect.' These special friendships often come to a sudden end, disrupted perhaps by the erotic feelings that often accompany them. Not having yet made the decisive turn towards heterosexual love, the young person may be disturbed by finding herself surreptitiously looking at or thinking about the friend in a sexual way.

Parents are sometimes disturbed by the intense attachment the adolescent forms with this friend, and may even feel jealous of the intimacy that was once theirs. But this identification with the idealised friend serves the same purpose as the child's earlier identification with parents, that is, to represent the missing perfection of the self, and thus protect self-esteem. Thus, if parents disapprove of a particular friend, it may be more useful to try to understand what desired quality he or she represents and try to help their adolescent to find more appropriate ways to achieve or express that quality.

Part of the adolescent search for identity is struggling to answer the question 'Who am I? A man or a woman?' The young adolescent has already taken significant steps towards answering that question. While the only way the pre-adolescent child can express the new sexual drive of puberty is by regressing to more infantile ways of getting pleasure, in early adolescence genital pleasure becomes the goal. The opposite sex assumes a new importance. The next big step will be falling in love. But in the meantime, the still largely unconscious bisexual preoccupations of early adolescence must be worked through by exploring these special idealised friendships, by having a rich fantasy life, by endless attention and care to the body. This is the time when parents are often horrified by finding art work or writings done by their teenagers which they consider weirdly erotic or disturbed. It is the time when young people often worry about their sexual orientation.

The eventual decline of the bisexual tendency marks the entrance to adolescence proper. The intensity of 'special' friendships and the pressure to conform to the peer group also wane at this time. By then, the adolescent's ideal self has become more firmly established in the personality and he or she does not need to 'live through' friends in the same way. This ideal self also gives the young person's life a new direction and sense of meaning — 'This is the kind of person I want to be'. Aware in a new way of their personal limitations, they have to bid farewell to the care-free megalomania of childhood. Faced at the same time with the monumental task of becoming an adult and making a mark in the world, young people could be easily crushed. The ideal self allows them to retain the missing perfection of the self, the possibility of completeness, and the energy and motivation to try to attain it.

Hunger for First Love — and Junk Food

The search for somebody to fall in love with, and the achievement of a secure sexual identity, shape much of the psychological development of adolescence proper. But before the new love can be found, the old childlike attachment to parents must be gradually relinquished. This process necessarily involves a withdrawal of some emotional energies from the parents, although they remain deeply significant for their adolescent children. Adolescents now deflect those freed-up emotional energies on to themselves. Thus, they become noticeably more egocentric or narcissistic during this phase of adolescence.

This narcissism is evident in the way adolescents tend to take themselves too seriously, to imagine themselves as the centre of the universe, to become very self-preoccupied, sometimes at the expense of other family members. In extremes, this self-preoccupation can cloud their judgment such that minor setbacks are perceived as major catastrophes. Another consequence of relinquishing the old childlike ties is that, before the new intimate ties of adulthood can take their place, a period exists when the ego is impoverished. There is a feeling of inner emptiness, of psychological hunger for attachment, which may be manifested in the almost greedy appetite of adolescents, their tendency to gorge food, which is not altogether related to their physical growth needs. Psychoanalyst Peter Blos observed that when adolescents fall in love, and thus satisfy their hunger for closeness, their oral cravings often abate.

Adolescents' intense self-absorption can make it seem that they are going backwards rather than forwards, becoming more childish rather than more mature. And indeed this can be a danger, especially for already vulnerable personalities, who may lose their grip on reality. Parents and friends may watch with mounting anxiety, as a child who was once merely 'insecure' or 'nerdy' becomes 'weird', unreachable, living in a world of his or her own.

Blos observed how hearing, seeing and touching can become exquisitely sensitive in adolescence, so that, caught up in fantasy, the adolescent often has trouble distinguishing what is happening inside the body from what is happening outside. The music seems to be speaking to them personally; they may feel an intense affinity with a particular singer or film star; random events are experienced as 'destiny'. They may develop strange superstitious rituals, believing that they can control the outcome of important events by wearing a specific item of clothing or following a particular routine.

One way that the adolescent tries to bridge inner and outer reality is by fantasy and creative activities which allow the expression of highly personal experiences and feelings in a way that other people, especially friends, can understand and relate to. Daydreaming and keeping a diary become common, allowing the young person to explore romantic and erotic fantasies, confused feelings, hopes and fears about the future. Creativity and artistic expression flower during this period.

It is in this phase of adolescence that the similarities with the second year of life become most apparent. Toddlers, newly aware of their separateness from the parent, struggle to achieve a sense of autonomy, an independent self. They do this in a characteristic way, by trial and error, by experimentation, testing the self by going to excess, by opposition.

In adolescence, this way of learning comes again to the fore. Adolescents too experiment with different identities — the soulful dreamer, the world-weary cynic, the tough guy, the vamp, the selfless hero. Fads, fashion, passionate attachments and infatuations are tried and discarded with dizzying speed. There is also inner experimentation, the testing-of-self by going to extremes, which is perhaps the most difficult for parents to understand and is often the cause of friction and tension in families.

The adolescent can veer from gorging on junk food to penitential diets; from self-preoccupation to intense idealism; from delicate sensitivity to emotional coarseness; from extreme sociability to moody withdrawal; from boundless optimism to utter dejection; from abject self-negation to extreme territoriality about every personal possession and opinion; from high-minded principles to petty argumentativeness; from high physical energy to lethargy.

Parents, irritated beyond endurance by these oscillations, can see no rational reason for such extremes and come to believe that this behaviour is simply designed to provoke them. But just as the toddler's 'boldness' is best understood as a growing and necessary self-assertiveness, the adolescent going to extremes is, according to Blos, a form of self-finding. Adolescents will almost wilfully work themselves up into states of excitement or exhaustion, mania or despair; they will seek extreme physical states and create heightened ego states by going to excess and extremes. These heightened states serve as an intense experience of self, of 'me', and thus serve to protect the boundaries of the as yet fragile ego.

This testing-of-self to extremes has another function. Just as newly walking toddlers discover their physical potential and limits by moving in every conceivable way — walking backwards, forwards, sideways, upside down — the adolescent, by experiencing physical and emotional extremes, gradually learns to understand control and inhibit impulses and actions. Gradually, this learning, this elaboration of the self, contains and channels the instinctual energies released by puberty.

The final development of this phase of adolescence occurs when the young person falls in love. Once this happens, there is a remarkable consolidation in sexual identity. Girls very often feel and act in a more traditionally feminine way, boys in a more traditionally masculine way. At the same time, they long for the lover to look and act like the opposite sex, to be a 'real' man or woman, to personify the parts of themselves that they now have to relinquish. Thus, falling in love signals the end of the bisexual position of earlier stages. For those young people who find that they are attracted to members of the same sex, this process of consolidating a sexual identity, of 'assigning' a complementary identity to the beloved has to be worked out in a more individual way, without the benefit or constraint of gender stereotypes. This process may be further burdened by the anxiety of not knowing whether their homosexuality is a permanent or a transitory phenomenon and the lack of a supportive context in which to discuss their concerns.

To adolescence proper, according to Blos, belongs the unique experience of tender love, that exquisite sense of longing for a beloved who (often on only the slightest acquaintance) is seen as the perfect object of desire, a delicate flower to be fiercely protected and adored. The adolescent in love surrenders to fantasies about the perfect, idealised encounter with the beloved. These fantasies bring with them a feeling of completeness that is deeply satisfying. At this stage there is still an internal conflict between the idealised feelings of love and the more disturbing erotic and sexual desire for the beloved — disturbing because falling in love resuscitates the old oedipal love of early childhood. Thus the experience of strong sexual desire is associated with a kind of oedipal guilt, a feeling that you have sullied the beloved with crude, carnal, illicit desires. Joyce, in *A Portrait of the Artist as a Young Man*, beautifully captures the conflict: 'A figure that had seemed to him by day demure and innocent came towards him by night through the winding darkness of sleep, her face transfigured by a lecherous cunning, her eyes bright with brutish joy.'

The revival of the oedipal conflict may also be manifested in other ways. The adolescent may be more physically affectionate to the parents, particularly the parent of the opposite sex, and simultaneously express disgust at the parent's body, smell and personal habits. There may also be an intensification of rivalry with the parent of the opposite sex, the adolescent describing to anybody who will listen just how pathetic the parent is and how they plan to run their lives and relationships in a much superior way when they are finally released from the tyranny of dependence on the self-same parents.

Meanwhile, they have to deal with those disturbing oedipal sexual feelings. Sometimes the experience of falling in love will provoke the adolescent into making an enormous effort to purify the self of all 'bad' habits, including masturbation. The adolescent may try to control all aspects of sensuality in an asceticism that is typical of adolescence: rigid regimes of diets, exercise, religious fervour and puritanical zeal of all kinds. In vulnerable personalities this asceticism may tip over into anorexia.

Gradually, the oedipal feelings are 'cleansed', worked through. The old libidinal tie with the parents of childhood is irrevocably transformed and there is a decisive turn towards a new beloved — real or imagined. Now, for the first time, the young person has the potential to connect those two great currents of affection and sexual desire into an adult-like love. This is a process that will not be completed for most until early adulthood. For young people whose family relationships are too insecure to withstand such psychological changes, this process may remain full of conflict and tension and they may bring these unresolved problems with them into their adult intimate relationships.

For the majority, great psychological development has been achieved by the end of adolescence. The momentous changes set in train by puberty have been integrated into the personality. The boy has become a man, the girl a woman. They have answered the burning question: 'Who am I?' — at least for now, and enough for them to say: 'I am set on the course of life. This is what I want to do. This is who I am. This is me.'

Am I a Boy or a Girl?

Adolescence has been described by the renowned psychologist Carol Gilligan as a uniquely problematical point in the psychological development of girls, a time when they are 'in danger of drowning or disappearing'. These are the stark terms used by a leading researcher to describe the struggle that breaks out in a girl's life at the edge of adolescence. The protected world of childhood suddenly comes to an end and she has to enter a new world that is governed by different rules. Her task is to forge a new identity as a young woman and to sort out vital issues relating to herself and her close relationships. And nowadays all this must be achieved within a culture that is hopelessly in conflict about what it wants of women, and is itself experiencing an unprecedented crisis about care and meaning in close relationships.

Small wonder then that girls are more likely to show psychological distress and to cope more poorly with stress in adolescence than at earlier stages of their development. Whereas in childhood it is boys who tend to respond more negatively to stress, this pattern is reversed during adolescence. Episodes of depression increase for girls; they show more disturbances in self-image and they are more disparaging about themselves, particularly their appearance, than are boys.

Freud believed that girls have a more difficult time because it is in adolescence that they have to resolve issues of sexual identity that boys have already partially resolved at an earlier stage. In psychoanalytical terms: to resolve the Oedipus complex, the young boy has to renounce his first identity with his mother, to give up his longing for her in the face of the rivalry of his stronger and more powerful father. To become a male, he has to identify with his father and thereby join the society of men. For a boy, the unremitting struggle to be masculine begins early.

The young girl, on the other hand, can stay identified and

attached to her mother throughout middle and late childhood. For her, the twin engines of psychological development — attachment and identity — can proceed in tandem. The issue of her sexual identity is not experienced as intensely or resolved as completely during childhood. For a girl to be described as 'a tomboy' never carries the same sense of shame as it does for a boy to be called as 'a sissy'. She can stay partially identified with her father in a way that the boy cannot stay identified with his mother.

Just at the onset of puberty, for both boys and girls, all the earlier resolutions of sexual identity are disturbed, and new, more mature identifications must be achieved. There is a resurgence of the unconscious bisexual identifications of infancy, characterised at the beginning of adolescence by increased sexual fantasy, a renewed interest in dirty jokes and heightened sexual curiosity.

Before taking the decisive step into a female identity, however, girls in the pre-teen years experiment intensely with the more striving, aggressive side of their nature. This is when playacting and tomboyishness reach their peak. It is the time when girls become 'horse-crazy', a preoccupation which psychoanalysts believe is a symbol of the girl's unconscious wish for phallic-like power.

This is the stage when girls are most likely to be described as 'bossy'. It is also a period which Gilligan found adolescent girls and women often look back on as a golden age: when they felt strong, full of their own opinions, stalwart resisters, outspoken companions. In the schoolyard, it is the girls in fifth or sixth class who chase the boys and who take the initiative in the early games of pseudo-love. The fact that the average girl between the ages of eleven and thirteen is taller than the average boy of the same age accentuates the girl's feelings of adequacy and power.

This is the world that the adolescent girl has to leave behind, temporarily, in her journey to become a woman. She has to struggle in a new way with the question 'Am I a boy or a girl?' — the theme intriguingly dealt with in Virginia Woolf's *Orlando*. The resolution of this bisexual preoccupation marks the girl's entry into adolescence proper.

The psychological task of adolescence, for boys and girls, is to develop a clear sense of self. For boys, the struggle is to break free, to psychologically separate from the parents. This is to some extent true for girls too, but for them, as always, identity is linked to attachment. The striving for independence is complicated by the fact that it must be accommodated within a more enduring aspect of identity — the central place of attachment and connection to others in her make-up. The conflict between these two opposing tendencies creates a major psychological dilemma for adolescent girls.

These psychological challenges are further complicated by the fact that a girl has to take on a cultural view of femininity that is itself in conflict about these same issues of attachment and independence. She has to engage with a traditional view of femininity that holds women to be responsible for caring in relationships, that equates female goodness with being selfless and self-sacrificing, being willing to subjugate her interests for another's happiness. If she takes on that version of femininity exclusively, she is immediately relegated to the second division and has to turn her back on the other more recent message to women: to be successful, you must be self-sufficient, independent, able to look after yourself.

In her struggle to survive in relationships, to be good and successful in the contradictory ways the culture expects, the adolescent girl finds herself caught on the horns of a dilemma: 'Is it better to respond to others and abandon myself or to respond to myself and abandon others?'

Thus, girls agonise about their relationships with their friends, their boyfriends and their parents — and especially with their mothers. They struggle for a genuine connection, a new place of entry into these relationships. They want to be known, seen, and most of all be heard, in a new way by those to whom they feel closest. The worst thing that can happen to adolescent girls is that people will stop listening and talking to them. They want to stay connected without capitulating to others.

Gradually, they learn the subtle psychological truth that a relationship implies being responsive to both self and others. They learn how to repair relationships by correcting the exclusion of their own concerns or the concerns of others. A strong sense of self in girls is found to be linked with the ability to solve such problems in relationships. That learning may, on occasion, make them moody, volatile and demanding. But they will emerge, at the end of that process, as strong young women, in no danger of psychologically drowning or disappearing.

Teenage Sex? Delay and Distract

Most parents anticipate their children's adolescence with apprehension. Fear for the safety of their increasingly independent teenagers and the associated fear of loss of control over them are the main reasons parents see adolescence as the most stressful stage of parenting. The research on teenage sexuality will not reassure them.

Surveys in America and Britain show that young people are initiated into sexual behaviour — kissing, cuddling, petting — at a younger age than ever before: fourteen years for girls, thirteen for boys. While the older generation waited on average for four years before progressing on to sexual intercourse, young people now do it after two years. Researchers have even documented the usual sequence of adolescent sexual behaviour: necking, feeling breasts through clothing, feeling breasts directly, feeling around the genital area, feeling the penis directly, intercourse. This all takes about two years. Now you know.

In Britain a quarter of all boys lose their virginity by age fifteen, and a half of them lose it by age seventeen. Nearly a fifth of girls have sexual intercourse before the age of sixteen. In America, the trend is more pronounced. By age fifteen, a third of boys and quarter of girls have had sex. By age nineteen, this has risen to 86 per cent for boys and nearly 80 per cent for girls.

Most of these adolescents had their first sexual experience in a steady relationship. More than two-thirds have sex again within six months of first intercourse. Most report that their first sexual experience 'just happened'. Other frequent explanations were: 'I was curious about what it would be like' and 'It seemed like a natural follow-on in the relationship.'

Despite the studied coolness of young people about sex, this revolution is high risk. Pregnancy and sexually transmitted diseases are real possibilities. Adolescents are confused about contraception, and the younger they are the less likely they are to take any precautions. Boys regard it as the girl's problem. In one study of sexually active teenage boys, only a third said they would be 'very upset' if the girl got pregnant, and less than a half said they would avoid intercourse if neither of them was using contraception.

Girls were somewhat better informed than boys about contraception. But for a third of sexually active girls, contraception meant no more than 'insisting on withdrawal'. Another third of these girls used no contraception. Not surprisingly, over a third of sexually active American teenage girls became pregnant within two years of first intercourse.

With such a revolution in adolescent sexual behaviour sweeping through most Western countries, can Ireland be far behind? What can parents do to protect their teenage children in this risky world of early, unprotected sex? Knowing some of the factors that precipitate young people into early sexual activity may be some help.

Social pressure from friends is identified by 73 per cent of American girls and 50 per cent of boys as a reason for early sex. Compared to their friends who are still virgins, teenage girls who are sexually active have been found to be more susceptible to pressure from boyfriends and to lack effective communication skills to cope with such sexual pressure.

Early puberty is another factor. Girls and boys who experience puberty earlier than their friends are more likely to be sexually active, especially if they are under a lot of social pressure to date members of the opposite sex. Of course, early puberty does not inevitably lead to early sex, but parents need to be aware that early puberty carries with it additional psychological hazards and that such adolescents need sensitive and supportive parenting to help them weather this storm.

Family circumstances also have an effect. For example, the sexual activity of teenagers is lowest in two-parent families, highest in single-parent families and in-between in remarried or 'blended' families. This may be because there is less parental supervision, owing to the pressures on single parents' time. Alternatively, if parents are themselves dating and are in a clearly sexual relationship, their own sexual behaviour may encourage their adolescent children to follow their lead. Or, in the aftermath of a family breakup, parents may be upset and preoccupied. Teenagers may feel psychologically stranded and look for comfort and intimacy outside the family. Whatever the family circumstances, parental vigilance and supervision of dating are vital. Early and steady dating is strongly related to early intercourse.

Greater communication with the mother is associated with less sexual activity and a greater use of contraception among teenagers. Interestingly, boys who discussed a large number of sexual topics with their fathers were more likely to be sexually active. Perhaps fathers who pride themselves on their sexual experience are not the best mentors for their sons.

The task of adolescence is the gradual relinquishment of childhood ties. But before the new intimate ties of an adult relationship can take their place, a period exists when the adolescent needs to return constantly to the safe haven of childhood. If parents cannot stay in close communication with their teenage children, the intense loneliness of these in-between years can precipitate the teenager into a premature, desperate bid for emotional security and affection in sexual intimacy.

Teenagers must be given the space and privacy to develop their own sexual lives. We must also accept that the development of any new behaviour involves a period of trial and error, but it is clear that for many teenagers this happens too early and without proper preparation. 'Delay' and 'distract' must be the key words for parents who want to help their children to cope with the pressures of early puberty and undue peer influence. Adolescents need structure in their lives. Creating a family atmosphere that encourages academic achievement, sports and creative pursuits provides them with a framework within which they can safely try out new things, experiment with new identities, and at the same time maintain continuity with the old pleasures of childhood.

Talking about Sex *With*, Not *At*, Teenagers

Having teenage children is enough to shake anybody's confidence, never more so than when you are attempting to talk to them about sex. There was a time when the problem was that parents did not have the right vocabulary. Now, with widespread media exposure to almost every aspect of sexuality, even the most reserved of parents are beginning to sound like Dr Ruth.

Many parents are still casting around for a formula for the best way to talk to their teenagers about sex. But the truth may be that there is none. Sex, ever subversive, refuses to be neatly bound by the structure of 'a talk'.

Even in the most enlightened families, the topic is difficult. Apart from anything else, where there are teenagers, whose burgeoning sexuality is newly defining them and their parents as sexual beings in each other's eyes, the incest taboo is strongly revived. Parents and children have to exclude their own sexual intimacy from the general intimacy of family life. Parents are rightly conscious of their teenagers' need for privacy and feel uncomfortable about intruding. For teenagers, in the grip of their own powerful sexual urges, the thought of their parents as sexual beings is too close for comfort. That is why they often convince themselves that their parents do not have sex anymore or if they do, it must be some geriatric version that bears no resemblance to their own real or fantasised experiences. Parents may attempt to get around the problem by trying to appear worldly-wise, approaching the topic like a close friend. Teenagers are alive to this subterfuge and head it off with a mixture of panic and pity: 'No offence, Dad, but nobody calls it that anymore ...'

Another reason the formula talk does not work is because very often it quickly turns into a version of the Redemptorists' Retreat in the 1950s. Worried parents may try to frighten their teenage children into responsible attitudes about sex, but warnings of potential dangers are often met with the standard adolescent response: 'It won't happen to me' or 'If it does happen to me, I can handle it.'

Adolescents tend to think of themselves as invincible, immune to the laws of life, death and statistical probability that govern us all. They are prepared to take all kinds of risks, falsely secure in the notion that they will never get sick, or caught or killed. That's not to say that all teenagers take big risks or do so very often. It is just that they deny these risks, and that is what unnerves parents.

But it would be a mistake to think of this adolescent 'fable of invincibility' as a deficit, a flaw to be attacked and criticised. Adolescents need that irrational surge of psychological energy to go out into the adult world, just as, when they were toddlers, they needed such prodigious physical energy to find out about the world.

Of course, parents need to inject their own experience of the world into those fantasies, but not in a way that will crush or cripple that energy, that will make their teenage children too frightened to risk emotional or physical intimacy.

The risks of AIDS and pregnancy are as nothing in the teenage mind compared to the fear that they will not grow up, that they will be left stuck at home, undesirable, uncool, rejected. In fact, fearing that their children will not eventually settle down into an independent life is often the biggest worry for parents of young adults. It is just that in the stresses of the adolescent years parents may forget about that long-term goal.

To reach independence, adolescents have to cross the great divide between childhood and adulthood. To stay in effective communication with them, parents must accompany their children on that journey. The psychological task for the adolescent is to progressively answer the questions 'Who am I? How am I the same as or different from those around me? What kind of a person am I going to be as an adult? To do this, adolescents have to experiment with different identities, by trial and error, by testing the limits, by opposition. They change, literally, by the day. The psychological task for parents is to stay involved enough in their children's lives so that they have some clue as to how those questions are being answered, while at the same time allowing their children room to grow. Too much involvement and the teenager will smother, too little and he or she will flounder.

Adolescents still desperately need their parents to be a safe haven. They can and should disengage only slowly from the emotional dependency of childhood. Recent studies show that even by late adolescence, parents continue to be the primary attachment figures for their children. Of those adolescents who said they had nobody to whom they could turn for comfort or on who they could depend for support, most were insecurely attached to their parents. They were the ones most likely to form intense romantic attachments at too early an age. The findings of other researchers are even starker. Adolescents who turn to premature sex may be lonely at home and desperate to be held and cuddled. Afraid that this will be considered childish, they settle instead for the grim bargain: sex as the price to be paid for a cuddle.

It is worth remembering that most research shows that parents have greater influence than peers on adolescents. The challenge is to exercise that influence in a way that fits in with the adolescent's growing up. Being grown up means having strong internal standards and a sense of self. These goals are best achieved by helping adolescents to develop insight into their own ideas and behaviour, to become more realistic and secure about themselves. And the way to do this is to listen and debate with them. Parents are too often perceived by teenagers as giving and justifying their own opinions, rather than listening.

In the long run, teenagers are most impressed by their parents' moral authority, most open to influence, when they see evidence of the parents' grasp of the situation, of their interest in taking the time to discuss the subtleties of relationships that count to their children. So if you find yourself talking about a recent teenage pregnancy or having an argument about the merits of contraception in the middle of driving your teenagers and their many friends to yet another party; if you know, without being told, why your teenager is down, if you are keeping up to date with the latest development with the best friend, then you do not need to worry about having big Talks about Sex.

Self-efficacy

Confidence: The Most Important Gift of All

Everybody wants to be competent, to do well what they should be doing in love and in work. They want to attract recognition and respect and feel satisfied with themselves. This is what psychologists call self-efficacy. But efficacy is not just a matter of knowing what to do or having the skills to do it. It is not even a matter of willpower. We may know full well what to do, but yet be unable to do it. To be competent, we also need the self-assurance to use our skills effectively, the belief that we can mobilise all our personal resources — our cognitive, social and behavioural skills — into effective courses of action to produce and regulate events in our lives. That is the critical mediator between knowing what to do and actually doing it.

How we judge our capabilities has profound effects on the way we act. People who are highly self-efficacious are usually successful in their lives because high perseverance usually produces high performance. What distinguishes them from their less successful counterparts is not ability or skill; it is their strong sense that they can withstand failure. They are not blindly optimistic. Rather, they attribute any uncertainty they may feel to the challenge of the task, and not as a fundamental doubt about their own capabilities. This is the subtle but vital distinction between high and low self-efficacy. The opposite of high self-efficacy is self-doubt.

Those who judge themselves to be low in self-efficacy approach tasks differently. They dwell on their personal deficiencies and imagine potential difficulties as more serious than they are. They torture themselves with visions of failure, leading to feelings of stress. This further impairs performance by diverting attention away from how best to proceed with the job to concerns about failure and mistakes. Those who are high in self-efficacy deal with uncertainty by investing a lot of effort in acquiring whatever knowledge and skills are required. In other words, their attention and effort are directed to the demands of the challenge. They are not overwhelmed by failure, but spurred to greater effort by obstacles.

Developing high or low self-efficacy is not a cool, rational process. Rather, feelings in general, particularly the manner in which fear and threat are handled, turn out to be very important. When facing a new or demanding situation, everybody has fears that things may go wrong. When we find that our fears are unfounded, our self-efficacy increases dramatically. The same thing happens when we confront the threatening situation and learn new skills to manage it. That is how we all learn self-efficacy.

If, however, in the course of completing a task we discover something intimidating about the demands, or something threatening to our way of doing things, our self-efficacy goes down, despite actually succeeding in completing the task. In such circumstances, the success leaves us feeling vulnerable rather than emboldened. Unless we can progressively learn to predict and manage potential threats, we shall not develop a robust self-assurance that will help us to master future tasks. Instead, we may falter and avoid future challenges altogether.

Probably the most interesting finding in all the research on self-efficacy is that people are more influenced by how they read their performance than by their actual successes. Repeated failures lower self-efficacy, particularly if they occur early in the course of events, or early in life. But persuasion and support have a very big influence on how success and failure are interpreted. People can give up trying because significant people in their lives seriously doubt that they can do what is required. They can come to believe that they are ineffectual, that it is their fault. A man once told me that his first memory of his father was of his saying 'I don't think you will ever amount to anything'. People are most likely to develop high self-efficacy when they have been set high standards and given the sense that they have the capacity to reach those standards.

Observing how others perform successfully or unsuccessfully also influences people's belief in themselves. The more we judge people to be close and similar to ourselves, the more powerful their influence on us, the more we use them as models. By repeatedly showing how difficulties are predictable and controllable, such a model can vicariously reduce stress for us and increase our preparedness to deal with threats in whatever situation might arise. Conversely, repeatedly seeing people who are important to us fail can undermine our self-efficacy, especially if we come to see them as quite similar to ourselves. For example, many difficulties experienced by young mothers, or by men in their midlife careers, may be due to suddenly finding themselves in a family or work situation that makes them fear that they will make the same mistakes as their own parents.

Developing high self-efficacy can also significantly influence our stress levels, how we recover from a variety of physical and psychological problems, such as heart attacks, panic attacks and phobias, and our ability to withstand pain. For example, people who believe that they can exercise some control over stressful events show less physiological arousal and impairment in performance than those who believe that they lack any personal control, even when both groups are subjected to the same stresses. It is the belief that you cannot cope that accounts for a lot of human distress. For example, people are physiologically undisturbed by tasks that they judge to be within their self-efficacy range. When they are moderately insecure about their efficacy, their heart rate accelerates and their blood pressure rises in anticipation of and during performance of the task. When tasks are so demanding that people avoid them, their heart rate falls, but their blood pressure continues to rise. However, when people are given help to raise their self-efficacy, they can face the same objectively difficult tasks without any physiological stress reactions.

While attempting to improve ourselves or others, most of us concentrate on acquiring or teaching new skills. Yet very often what comes between us and our optimal functioning is not skill deficit. Rather, the problem is lack of confidence to act on our capabilities, poor self-knowledge, and faulty internal standards in how success and failure are measured. Many women already know that. That is why they are so interested in self-development. Perhaps when somebody relabels self-development as training in emotional competence, men will finally start taking it seriously.

How can self-efficacy be increased? Much can be learned from clinical work. A high sense of self-efficacy, combined with a responsive environment that rewards performance and achievement, produces people who are assured and competent in their work and emotional lives. A high sense of self-efficacy, combined with an unreasonable or punitive environment will produce people who do not necessarily give up, but whose energies are diverted into managing feelings of grievance, resentment or permanently rebelling and protesting. A low sense of self-efficacy, combined with an environment that is responsive to others, but not to you, tends to produce people who feel ineffectual, despondent, depressed and self-critical. Finally, low self-efficacy, combined with an environment that is unrewarding to anybody, no matter what their efforts, produces people who are apathetic and resigned to failure.

In clinical work, people are helped to identify the emotional and behavioural cues in themselves and in the environment which they are often, unconsciously, responding to. Once identified, these cues can come under some conscious control, evaluation and choice. The key to increasing self-efficacy is to identify the cues in ourselves and in the environment which we have learned to use as signs of personal efficacy.

Many people seriously underestimate their own capabilities. This can arise because of faulty self-knowledge, consistent errors in the way challenging tasks are evaluated or, most frequently, particular maladaptive ways of dealing with feelings of threat and failure. For example, those low in self-efficacy have much more trouble giving up any addictive behaviour, like smoking or drug-taking because they are more likely to attribute a slip to chronic problems in themselves, leading them to give up trying to cope with the addiction and to a breakdown in self-control. Studies have shown, for example, that neither demographic factors, smoking history or degree of physical dependence on nicotine differentiated relapsers from successful abstainers. Rather it was the degree of self-efficacy. At the end of various courses of treatment, it was the person's own perceived self-efficacy that predicted months later who would relapse, how soon they would relapse, and even the specific situations in which they would slip.

People with high self-efficacy are distinguished from those with low self-efficacy not by their superior knowledge or skills, but by their ability to predict and cope with the possibility of failure. That is the paradox of success. Clearly, then, understanding how we react to failure is important. What do we perceive as the causes of our failures? There are three ways we answer that question. Do we see failure as the result of personal or external factors? Do we see the causes of failure as being enduring or transient? Do we believe that the causes operate in many situations or only in a few? Those who are low in self-efficacy tend to answer these questions in this way: 'My failures are due to this particular deficiency or fault in me, which will always be with me and will affect me in whatever situation I find myself.' Those high in self-efficacy will tend to answer the question this way: 'My failure was due maybe to this particular deficiency, but it was also due to the particular situation I found myself in. Next time I will be better prepared and try harder. Anyway, I usually perform better in the following circumstances ...'

For those with low self-efficacy, the solutions may be to identify new knowledge to be learned and skills to be mastered. But rarely. The solutions are most often in changing the internal standards by which success and failure are measured. Stringent internal standards of success, the classic perfectionism, turn objective successes into personal failures and make avoidance and stagnation less painful than devalued partial successes. In clinical work, the person is helped to set goals towards a measured success and is encouraged to base evaluations on internal comparison, on a personal standard, that is, from where you started, rather than comparison with some objective measure of success. They are taught to reward themselves psychologically, to 'parent' themselves if you like, in the way they expected or wished that their actual parents or superiors reacted to them.

They are taught to attend to what is familiar and clearly within their competence in a new task, rather than on what is strange; to re-examine failures with compassion, as the most important learning experiences. Most importantly, they are encouraged to believe that self-efficacy is not about the kind of striving that leaves you drained before you start. Rather, it is taking responsibility for becoming the person you always, somewhere in your heart, believed you could be.

How Feelings Count

It is axiomatic that most women are interested in feelings: how they develop, how they affect us, how they change. But feelings are about to cross the gender gap. Men, and the world they live in, are about to discover what women have always known; that feelings are important for how we conduct ourselves in relationships at home, at work and in society.

But while women are content to talk about feelings in terms of self-development, men prefer to think about feelings in terms of competencies or skills, thus perhaps lending this rather soggy realm a certain gravitas and seriousness of purpose to which men find it easier to relate.

Thus, Daniel Goleman's controversial new book *Emotional Intelligence* will hit the right note with many men, and, of course, reassure us women that we have, after all, been on the right track. On the basis of the now extensive research on emotional functioning, Goleman proposes that there are in effect two brains, two minds, two ways of knowing. One is the rational brain, traditional intelligence, knowing by thinking and reasoning. The other is the emotional brain, the impulsive, powerful, sometimes illogical way of knowing.

These two minds, the emotional and the rational, operate in tight harmony and reflect two distinct but interconnected circuitries in the brain; because of the basic architecture of mental life, the emotional centres have immense power to influence the functioning of the rest of the brain.

Research has shown, for example, that in the first few milliseconds of perceiving something, we not only unconsciously comprehend what it is, but decide whether we like it or not. Our emotions have a mind of their own, one that can hold views quite independent of our rational mind and even overwhelm it. More interesting still, it is actually impossible to make decisions based on pure reason.

Goleman cites research done by neurologist Antonio Damasio on people whose brains are damaged in a way that severs the connection to the emotional memory. Despite the fact that such individuals show no deterioration in IQ or any cognitive ability, they make disastrous choices in business and in their personal lives, and can vacillate endlessly over a simple decision like when to make an appointment.

What this book argues is that, far from trying to ignore or suppress emotions, as if they are an impediment to reason, what is now required is to firmly place the intelligence of emotions centre stage in our understanding of human nature and our vision of excellence. Consider the following.

When ninety-five Harvard University graduates were followed into middle age, the men with the highest intelligence test scores in college were found not to be particularly successful, compared to those who had scored lower, in terms of salary, productivity, or status in their chosen field. Neither did they have the greatest satisfaction, nor the most happiness in their personal relationships. At best, IQ seems to contribute only about 20 per cent to the factors that determine life success, leaving 80 per cent to other forces.

Many psychologists now believe that emotional intelligence is a key sub-set of those 'other forces' — a concept first articulated by Peter Salovey of Yale University in 1990. He expanded the traditional view of intelligence into five emotional domains:

> **Knowing your emotions**. Self-awareness — recognising a feeling as it happens — is the keystone of emotional intelligence, crucial for psychological insight and confidence about decision-making.
> **Managing emotions**. This includes the ability to soothe yourself, to shake off debilitating negative feelings and to bounce back from adversity.
> **Motivating yourself**. This includes the ability to marshal emotions in the service of a goal and, most importantly,

emotional self-control. Being able to delay gratification and to control impulsiveness underlies achievement of all kinds. **Recognising emotions in others**. Empathy is the fundamental 'people skill', that is, the ability to be attuned to the subtle social signals that indicate what other people need. **Handling relationships**. This is the ability to manage emotions in others, and is what underlies leadership, popularity and interpersonal effectiveness.

People can differ in their abilities in each of these domains. And how adept a person is in each is crucial to understanding why one person succeeds in life, while another of equal or greater intelligence fails. The research of Walter Mischel demonstrates how important just one of those emotional competencies is; that is, the ability to delay gratification.

Mischel conducted an experiment with a class of four-year-olds. He gave each of them a marshmallow and told them they could eat it immediately. However, if they could resist eating it until the experimenter came back from running an errand, he would then give them two marshmallows. For what must have seemed like an endless fifteen minutes, most of the children waited.

In their struggle to resist the marshmallow, they resorted to putting their hands over their eyes, they talked to themselves, sang, played games with their hands and their feet, they even tried to go to sleep. About a third of the children, more impulsive, were unable to resist the temptation. They grabbed the marshmallow, almost always within seconds of the experimenter leaving the room.

The diagnostic power of how that moment of impulse was handled became clear when these same children were followed up and again assessed as teenagers. Those who at four had been able to resist temptation were, as adolescents, more socially competent and personally effective. They were better able to cope with frustration, less likely to become rattled by stress. They sought out challenges and did not give up on them even when faced with difficulties. They were self-reliant, dependable and confident, and still able to delay gratification in pursuit of their goals.

The children who at four had been unable to resist temptation seemed more psychologically troubled, more socially isolated, stubborn, indecisive, upset by frustrations, prone to jealousy and getting into conflict with others, less confident. They still had great difficulty putting off gratification in pursuit of their goals.

When these adolescents were again tested as they were finishing secondary school, those who had been able to delay gratification at four were found to be superior as students to the one-third who had given in to temptation, and had dramatically higher scores on tests of verbal and mathematical ability.

How children reacted to the marshmallow test at age four was twice as powerful a predictor of their test results at the end of secondary school as their IQ at age four (which becomes a stronger predictor only after children learn to read). This suggests that the ability to delay gratification contributes powerfully to intellectual potential, quite apart from IQ itself. Or, if you like, given roughly the same range of intellectual abilities, emotional aptitudes make the critical difference.

Take optimism, for example — another 'master aptitude' that can determine not just academic but corporate success. In a study of insurance salesmen at the MetLife company in the United States, psychologist Martin Seligman showed the power of optimism to motivate high work performance. This company had a problem. Selling insurance is a difficult job, the ratio of successful to unsuccessful sales being depressingly low. As a consequence, about three-quarters of insurance salesmen leave the job in their first three years. Given the high costs of recruiting and training a sales force of several thousand, the emotional state of their employees became an economic issue for the company.

Seligman found that new salesmen who were natural optimists sold 37 per cent more insurance in their first two years on the job than did salesmen who were pessimists. And during the first year, the pessimists left at twice the rate of the optimists. He persuaded MetLife to hire a special group of applicants who scored high on a test of optimism, even though they had failed the normal screening procedures used by the company. This special group outsold the pessimists by 21 per cent in their first year and by 57 per cent in the second.

Why was optimism an emotionally intelligent aptitude in that situation? Because the way a salesman emotionally explains his successes and failures is crucial to the ability to marshal enough motivation to continue and to try harder the next time. People who are pessimists explain failures as due to some lasting characteristic in themselves or in others which they are helpless to change. Optimists, on the other hand, explain failures as due to something temporary that can be changed. So they believe they can succeed the next time round.

For example, pessimists typically respond to set-backs like 'feeling run down' by saying 'I never get a chance to relax', whereas optimists are more likely to define it as a short-term problem, such as 'I have been exceptionally busy.'

Thus, a series of failed sales will be explained by a pessimist as 'I'm a failure at this', but by the optimist as 'I must be using the wrong approach' or 'that last customer was just in a bad mood'. As Seligman's study demonstrated, each reaction has profound implications for how actively and effectively the salesman will tackle future selling.

Companies, under increasing pressure to transform their organisation structures away from rigid authoritarian hierarchies into small, flexible, team-based working arrangements, are having to put a new premium on the interpersonal competence of their employees. In the words of one Harvard Business School psychologist, quoted by Goleman: 'the virtuoso in interpersonal skills is the corporate future'.

Robert Sternbert, the Yale psychologist, found that what made some work teams far more effective than others was what he called 'group intelligence', which turned out not to be the average 'group IQ' in the academic sense, but 'group emotional intelligence', especially the ability to create social harmony. In other words, a team composed of individuals who are intelligent in the traditional sense, who are verbally fluent and technically skilled, may collectively act 'stupidly' if they are not able to manage the group dynamic.

In teams where there are high levels of emotional and social static — arising from fear, unresolved conflict, rivalries and resentments — the individual talents of the group members will be largely wasted.

Yet there remains in the world of work a lingering ambivalence about acknowledging that managing feelings can be as important a task as investing in new technology or balancing the budget. One study of executives and white collar workers showed, for example, that they ranked inept criticism as a more frequent cause of conflict on the job than mistrust, personality struggles and disputes over power and pay.

Another study of 250 executives found that most felt that their work demanded 'their heads but not their hearts'. Many said that they feared that feeling empathy for those they worked with would put them in conflict with their organisational goals and would make it impossible to deal with people.

Others believed that if they were not emotionally aloof, they would be unable to make the hard decisions that business requires. Clearly, if companies want to boost their corporate emotional intelligence, there will need to be a revolution in attitudes such as these. But perhaps the best way to the male corporate heart is through the physical heart. The kind of negative emotions stirred up by poorly managed interpersonal relations can be toxic for your health. People who experience chronic anxiety or hostility, relentless cynicism or suspiciousness have double the risk of diseases such as asthma, arthritis, ulcers and heart disease. There are now dozens of studies that show that anger is particularly dangerous for your heart. When patients who had one first heart attack recounted incidents that made them angry, the pumping efficiency of their hearts dropped by five percentage points, making it a particularly lethal emotion for those who already have heart disease.

For women, on the other hand, the more deadly emotion may be anxiety and fear. But if some emotions can be toxic, there are others that are more healing. For example, when 122 men who had suffered a heart attack were followed up eight years later, those who had demonstrated a positive and optimistic attitude after their heart attack were found to have done much better than their more pessimistic counterparts. In fact, their mental outlook proved a better predictor of survival than any medical risk factor, including the amount of damage to the heart in the first place, artery blockage, cholesterol level or blood pressure.

Thomas Kuhn, in his landmark book *The Structure of Scientific Revolutions*, showed that almost every significant breakthrough in science involved a break with the traditional ways of thinking. As Daniel Goleman shows in this book, there is now enough psychological evidence accumulated to question the old paradigm that the world must revolve only around the sun of rational, analytical knowledge. It is now time for a paradigm shift that places emotions, alongside reason, in the centre of the universe. Or, put more simply, feelings count.

Hold on Fast to Your Illusions

It used to be thought that being in contact with reality, that is, having an accurate perception of yourself, the world and the future, was the hallmark of mental health. Not so, it seems. There is now evidence to show that three illusions — having an overly positive view of yourself, an exaggerated sense of control, and an unrealistically optimistic attitude — are characteristic of the well-functioning individual. Such illusions seem to enable people not just to be personally contented and happy, but to care better for others and to engage in productive and creative work.

Psychologists have now amassed more than a decade's research to show that most people, when asked to describe themselves, focus on their positive side; show much poorer recall of their failures than their successes; and when engaged in joint work, tend to attribute successful outcomes more to themselves than to their partner. Even when negative aspects of the self are acknowledged, they tend to be dismissed as inconsequential and common failures, whereas the positive aspects of the self are regarded as rare and distinctive. In experimental learning situations, people think they have improved on abilities that are important to them, even when their performance in fact has remained unchanged. There is a pervasive and ultimately healthy tendency to vanity, to see ourselves as better than others.

But what about people who have a realistic and balanced view of their good and bad points? Surely they must rank among the most successful and fulfilled? Alas, no. Balanced and objective individuals form the legions of the mildly depressed. People who accurately perceive their own faults and shortcomings, who have no difficulty recalling their poor performances and failures, who are even-handed in attributing successes to the efforts of others as well as themselves (as opposed to normal people who tend to claim the lion's share of the credit for themselves) are more psychologically distressed and have lower self-esteem.

We also apparently harbour illusions about the amount of control we have over events. In a series of ingenious experiments, psychologists show that well-functioning people often act as if they can control situations that are determined by chance and are totally outside their influence. In one experiment using a type of gambling machine, individuals attributed their occasional successes to factors such as skill, personal control and involvement when they were, in fact, due to chance. There were those, of course, who were not taken in by this illusion of control. They were more accurate in estimating their degree of influence. Guess who? Those who were depressed, or in whom the experimenters had induced a negative mood before the experiment.

In much the same way, most of us hold what, in strictly logical terms, is an overly warm and generous view of what the future will bring us personally. For example, we believe that, compared to our peers, we have a better chance of getting a satisfying, well-paid job or of having a gifted child. We also choose to believe that we are less likely to have a car accident, be a crime victim or get sick. Again, it is only the mildly depressed and those with low self-esteem who have a more realistic and balanced assessment of their likely future circumstances.

What kills illusions, and what is bad for our psychological health, is the kind of painstaking, unblinking self-consciousness of the 'I'm always trying to figure myself out' variety. This is the kind of psychological stance which never allows threatening or negative information to be screened out. The value of our illusions about our own capabilities and the prospects for the future may be that they create self-fulfilling prophecies. They allow us to disregard the objectively poor probabilities for success that exist in many situations that might otherwise stop us even trying. Our positive illusions allow us to lift off, to try harder and longer, and to reinterpret the inevitable failures as learning experiences.

Subjecting yourself to the scrutiny of cold reality at the beginning of a challenging task is not psychologically helpful. It is psychologically crippling. It is like a parent who makes such devastatingly accurate judgments on a child's efforts that the child is overwhelmed by just how powerless, ignorant and immature he or she is. What is required, rather, is the art of compassion, to look on the child, and ourselves, with a loving eye.

In therapy, this can be done by getting people to change the internal standards against which they measure success and failure. Overly stringent internal standards, classic perfectionism, tend to turn objective success into personal failure and have the effect of making avoidance and stagnation preferable to effort. Part of the solution is to set intermediate goals, and to learn to base evaluations of achievement on a personal standard, rather than on some objective measure. The idea is to focus on the distance travelled from the starting point, rather than on the distance from the goal.

Reaction to failure is important. Those who are low in self-esteem tend to think: 'My failures are due to this particular deficiency or fault in me, which will always be with me and will affect me in whatever situation I find myself.' In contrast, those high in self-esteem tend to circumscribe the problem, to throw a psychological cordon around it: 'My failure was due maybe to a particular deficiency in myself, but it was also due to the particular situation I found myself in. Next time I will be better prepared and try harder. Anyway, I usually perform better in the following circumstances …'

If your self-esteem is low, you must learn to reward yourself psychologically, to take a more indulgent view of yourself and your achievements, just as you wish your parents had. You must go against your deepest instincts to be self-critical, and instead give yourself the benefit of the doubt. Allow yourself the normal illusions — and you may stop being mildly depressed all the time.

Taking Charge of Life at Work

All of us from time to time have had the experience of being in control of our actions, in charge of our lives. The accompanying feelings of exhilaration and deep enjoyment serve as a bench- mark for what life should be like. These are what psychologists call peak or optimal experiences. Psychologist Mihaly Csikszentmihalyi of the University of Chicago has spent twenty- five years investigating this elusive phenomenon and has devel- oped a theory of optimal experience based on the concept of 'flow' — the state in which people are so involved in an activity that nothing else seems to matter; the experience itself is so enjoyable that people will do it even at great cost, just for the sake of doing it.

Research with thousands of people worldwide has demon- strated that optimal experiences — what Csikszentmihalyi calls 'flow' — are described in the same way by men and women, young and old, regardless of social class or cultural differences. The experience is universal in the sense that it is not confined to particular activities. For example, people report experiences of optimal functioning while performing major surgery, doing rou- tine assembly-line work, playing chess, reading to a child, swarming around in a motor-cycle gang, and surviving great adversity. In other words, people can experience deep enjoyment or 'flow' while carrying out a wide variety of things, but the sub- jective psychological experience tends to be described in almost identical terms.

People mention at least one and often all the following when they describe optimal experience or 'flow': the experience occurs when they take on tasks they have a chance of completing; they are fully concentrated on what they are doing; that concentration is possible because the task has clear goals and provides an immediate response. They often act with a deep but effortless involvement that removes from their awareness the frustrations and worries of everyday life; they feel a sense of control over what they are doing; concern for the self or self-consciousness disappears, yet, paradoxically, they feel stronger in themselves and more self-confident after the 'flow' experience is over. Lastly, the sense of time is altered: hours seem to pass in minutes, but also minutes in some circumstances can seem to stretch into hours. The combination of all these elements produces such a profound sense of enjoyment that people do not count the cost of the time and energy they expend.

The vast majority of optimal or 'flow' experiences are not sudden, spontaneous feelings of well-being. Rather, they occur during the course of activities — work or leisure — that are goal-directed and bounded by rules. In other words, they are not passive experiences in a state of relaxation, but are the result of consciously undertaken activities that require a significant investment of psychological energy or attention and could not be done without acquiring appropriate skills. The challenge, though initially taxing or even negative, turns into enjoyment at a very particular point: when the individual perceives that the opportunity for action is equal to his or her capabilities, that is, at the boundary between boredom (when the task is too simple) and anxiety (when the task is too complex).

When that balance between opportunity and competence is reached, attention is absorbed by the activity. There is no excess psychological energy left over to process any other information. People become so involved in what they are doing that the activity appears to be almost automatic. People in 'flow' stop being aware of themselves as separate from the actions they are performing. Though the movement appears effortless, it is in fact highly disciplined physical or mental activity, frequently both. Any lapse in concentration will destroy the feeling of 'flow'. In contrast to the execution of routine activities, where we may be plagued by doubts, uncertainties and distractions ('Why am I doing this? Should I be doing something else?'), 'flow' experiences are characterised by the expenditure of what Erik Erikson calls 'unconflicted energy' — the essence of mental well-being.

Clarity of goals and immediate response to performance are critical. Indeed, one of the most significant implications of the research is that optimal functioning, and ultimately happiness, are possible only if an individual has learned to set attainable goals for him- or herself and to use feedback effectively. The resulting capacity to focus attention on the task in hand imposes an order on consciousness and excludes from awareness all those stray, random and negative events (such as pain, anger, feelings of being threatened) that undermine optimal psychological functioning.

In ordinary life, we are constantly processing all the information that we allow into our awareness. When such information is in line with what we want to do, we feel empowered. Our energy is released and we experience a sense of inner harmony. To the extent that our thoughts, feelings, senses and intentions are all focused on the same goal, we feel 'together', in control and productive. However, when we become aware of information that conflicts with our intentions (for example, worries about failure or losing control), our energy becomes distracted, unwieldy and ineffective. We become unproductively self-conscious. The more we can achieve positive control over our attention — that is, over what we allow into consciousness, over our attention — the more we can take charge of our inner life and therefore our happiness.

Perhaps the most mysterious aspect of 'flow' is the loss of self-consciousness. This is often associated with a feeling of union with some bigger presence. The yachtsman may begin to experience himself as 'at one' with the boat, the sea and the elements. The surgeon may experience an intense feeling of oneness with the operating team, the painter with nature. Yet, paradoxically 'flow' involves a very active awareness of self in another sense. A good athlete in 'flow' is usually aware of every muscle, every breath, every other relevant competitor. What slips below awareness is a kind of distracting self-preoccupation, for example, worrying about how we appear to others. For a while, we are freed from the babble of our consciousness and we come back feeling that we have transcended ourselves, pushed out the boundaries of what we are. So we end up feeling both more ourselves and at the same time belonging to a bigger presence.

The more time a person reports experiences of 'flow' in their average week, the more likely they are to describe themselves as strong, active, creative, concentrated and motivated. In a culture increasingly preoccupied by 'quality of life', and increasingly dependent on a motivated and creative workforce, the implications of the research on 'flow' could be far-reaching. Potentially, the world of work could be transformed if jobs were redesigned to allow for more frequent 'flow' experiences.

More important, it would also require helping people develop the psychological skills to control consciousness — the ability to transform problems into challenges, to set appropriate goals for self, to accurately use the information they get on their performance, to develop disciplined attention and concentration, and to enjoy immediate experience. If this sounds like self-development, that's exactly what it is. But far from being a perk, the evidence suggests that a great deal of productive creativity, presently dissipated, would be released if self-development became part of the work agenda.

Armed for Real-life Conflict

If you were asked to describe the most stressful experiences you have had in the last year — in your work or personal relationships — it is probable that an unresolved or badly handled conflict will feature prominently in many of those experiences. A negative outcome to conflict can leave you feeling angry, betrayed, depressed and with lowered self-esteem. At a deeper level, you may feel disconnected from your deeply held desires and needs, thrown off course. In cases of severe conflict, your energy can become trapped in defensive manoeuvres and you may feel unable to move forward.

On the other hand, if you were asked to describe experiences that helped you to value yourself more, it is probable that they will include conflicts that you handled creatively and well. A positive outcome to conflict can result in feelings of expansion, change, joy, a heightened self-efficacy, a sense of moving on to a new level.

Clearly, conflict resolution skills constitute a core competency. Not just are they central to self-esteem, they are essential for productive work and well-functioning relationships. In a world that is increasingly concerned with equal, non-hierarchical personal relationships and with giving people a voice in the decisions that affect their lives, such skills are critical for dealing with the inevitable differences that arise between people. The ability to negotiate is key to a well-functioning democracy — at home, at work, and in the community at large. Yet very few of us receive any formal education or training in negotiation.

The traditional response to resolving conflict is for each side to take a position, argue for it and then make concessions to reach a compromise. Sometimes the agreements are satisfactory, sometimes not. The problem is that, from early on, each side becomes locked into their respective positions. You try to improve your chances by starting with an extreme position, sticking to it and making as few concessions as possible. This all takes a lot of time and a surfeit of decisions (what to offer, what to reject, how much of a concession to make). Each time you concede, you are afraid it will create more pressure to concede further.

You have to convince the other side that it will be impossible for them to change your position. However, the more you become committed to doing that, the more impossible it will become for you to change without losing face. The same is true for the other side. Egos become involved, and whenever egos become involved, there's trouble. In fact, very often the original problem is entirely lost sight of and the parties become locked in a battle of wills, preoccupied with not losing face.

More gentle souls adopt a softer negotiating style in order to preserve a good relationship with the other party. They readily make offers and concessions, yielding as necessary to avoid confrontation. This style can work well if both parties have a similar stance. However, if the other side takes a harder stance, it opens up the possibility of exploitation of the softer bargainer.

The Harvard Negotiation Project* has pioneered an alternative way to resolve differences, a method of reaching constructive agreements that the three authors call 'principled negotiation', which can be applied as an all-purpose strategy to any negotiation.

The first element of principled negotiation involves separating the people from the problem. Despite almost all our experience to the contrary, we persist in believing that resolving differences can be done exclusively by reason. Each time we run up against incomprehensible misunderstandings, tangled communication, and what appear to be wildly irrational feelings, we register child-like shock. We forget that the people negotiating (including ourselves) are emotional. That is why the first tenet of principled negotiation is to ask yourself at every point of the negotiation 'Am I paying enough attention to the people problem?'

*The Project has published widely. Its best known book is *Getting to Yes: Negotiating Agreement without Giving In* by Roger Fisher, William Ury and Bruce Patton (Penguin Books, 1991).

Most negotiations take place with people with whom you already have a relationship. Thus, there is not just the issue of difference to be resolved, but there is also the need to take care of the relationship. If the negotiation becomes a battle of wills, the possibility of a good relationship in the future may be traded off against the temporary pleasure of getting your own way. Psychological issues must be dealt with by psychological means. Hence the necessity to deal with people's perception of what is going on. Ultimately, it does not matter whether the other party's fears, hopes and grievances are 'objectively' true or not. You must engage directly with reality as that person sees it. Facts alone will not solve the problem. To do that, you have to fully understand their thinking or, even better, to feel some sympathy for their point of view. The Harvard group identified the ability to put yourself in the other's shoes as one of the most important skills a negotiator can possess.

Another key skill is the ability to avoid blaming the other. Even if justified, blaming is usually counterproductive; it uses up your energy and blunts your judgment. You may be so busy blaming that you miss subtle changes in the other side's position. It also makes the other party defensive and determined to resist what you have to say.

Feelings may be more important than talk in a negotiation. It is important to allow for the expression of strong feelings, though they appear to be slowing up the process. That means learning how to listen fully to negative feelings, even if they are directed at you, and learning not to react to emotional outbursts in a way that highlights the negative cycle. Acknowledging the strength of the person's feelings and apologising, without necessarily admitting personal responsibility for the grievance, can do much to defuse angry feelings and open up the possibility of better communication about solutions ('I understand much better now how strongly you feel about this. I'm really sorry that you feel so hurt and badly treated. This has helped to clear the air.')

There is no cost for such sympathy. The person who can respond like that is not being bullied or got the better of, but is actually taking the initiative. The result is that he or she will feel more in control of the situation. In fact, both parties generally feel better about themselves after such an interaction. Yet there are a great many people in organisations and marriages who are so caught up in managing their own negative feelings that they are unable to see, let alone acknowledge, the other person's negative feelings. As a consequence, what may start as a small issue, involving only a minor personal or financial cost, can grow into a tension that can permanently undermine or even destroy the relationship.

If you take the other party seriously, they are more likely to reciprocate and take into account your personal concerns. For example, if the settlement is going to cause you lot of personal inconvenience, this issue, instead of being labelled in a derogatory way ('All you're interested in is your own convenience'), becomes an issue to be taken seriously and cared about. Empathy makes it more likely that both parties will see each other as partners, facing a common problem, rather than as adversaries.

Discovering basic interests

A good agreement is one that will satisfy the legitimate interests of both parties in a negotiation. Only in that way can both sides live with it. Yet our tendency is to stick to negotiating positions which often obscure what we really want. Discovering the basic interests underlying positions is not easy. But, generally, the most powerful interests are basic human needs, such as feeling appreciated, secure, in control of your life and so on. If these needs are threatened (or perceived to be threatened), there is unlikely to be much progress in solving any conflict. As long as you are willing to listen to the basic concerns of the other party, you can afford to communicate yours directly and with feeling.

Roger Fisher, William Ury and Bruce Patton of the Harvard Negotiation Project consider that focusing on interests rather than stated positions is a key element in securing good agreements.

The core problem in a negotiation is the conflict between each side's interests, that is, their needs, desires and fears. These interests are what cause people to adopt positions. Thus, concentrating on stated positions is just skating on the surface. It is more effective to try to discover your own and the other party's underlying interests because what you may then discover is that, despite having opposing positions, you may also share some basic interests.

For example, if your husband does not want you to go to your mother's, it may not be because he does not care about pleasing you, but because he is concerned that the visit will upset you or because he wants to spend more time with you. Once you don't feel under attack, you may be free to acknowledge that you also feel anxious about the effect of the visit on yourself and have an interest in spending more time with your husband. Of course, he may also not like your mother, but in the context of the underlying interests that you share, the actual disagreement about this visit may be more manageable. Once you stay focused on basic interests, not positions, you can usually come up with several ways that your interests and those of the other side can be met.

Part of the skill in doing this is not to start by stating your solution, however obvious it is to you. Instead, start by saying what your interests are and how the problem is affecting them. The other party will then be more likely to listen, if only to see where the discussion is leading. You carry the other party with you in the discussion, as it were, so that when you come to your proposal, they will understand where you are coming from. If you start by stating your solution (which almost certainly requires them to make a change) and then go on to give your arguments for it, the chances are that the other party will already be preparing counter-arguments and not listening to your reasoning.

One of the most important insights of the Harvard group was that if you ask people why they are arguing, their answer will typically identify a cause ('He did not do what I asked him to do'), not a purpose ('We are trying to figure out how to improve communication'). Caught up in the quarrel, they are more likely to keep reacting to what the other side has said or done than to pursuing their own long-term interests.

Interests are better served if you talk about where you would like to go, what you would like to happen, rather than where you have come from. This insight fits in with the standard therapeutic technique in relationship counselling: helping each partner to restate grievances as positive requests.

Another element of good negotiation involves inventing options for mutual gain. In many conflicts, people get locked into 'zero-sum thinking': there's a right answer (my solution) and a wrong answer (your solution). If you win, I lose. There are usually many solutions to a problem, but people are often afraid that generating many different ideas will only delay the process or make it unclear. But wise solutions take time and are very rarely the most obvious ones. Most crucially, a good agreement must appeal not only to your self-interest, but to the self-interest of the other side.

A good agreement must be one with which each side can live. The key is to make it easy for them to come to the decision you want. Thus, it is important to frame your proposal in a way that gives them some choice between different, equally acceptable options and that requires only a simple decision to accept. Conversely, it is not helpful to frame your proposal in a way that leaves the other party feeling boxed-in ('It's this or nothing') or nervous about the limits of your demand ('Come up with something and I'll see if that is enough').

The final element is insisting on using objective criteria. No matter how well you understand the other side's position, or how well you manage the relationship, the stark reality of conflicting interests remains. Settling this by a battle of wills will be costly to the relationship. Mechanically splitting the difference may end in an agreement that pleases neither party. An alternative is to negotiate on the basis of agreed objective criteria. Energy is then concentrated on finding and agreeing on such criteria, rather than on breaking the will of the other side.

This is the main strategy that mediators use when helping couples come to workable agreements about the end of their relationship. Most individuals like to think of themselves as fair and, even when they are upset and angry, are more willing to agree to things on that basis rather than to exhortations that this is what they should have done in the first place. A solution based on the first will be experienced as an opportunity to demonstrate their good nature or character, the latter as a defeat.

If each side is reassured that the final outcome will not be binding unless they are confident that it is fair, this gives them a basis to enter negotiation, even when trust has broken down between them. An additional assurance is provided if they are asked to negotiate a fair agreement before they go on to decide their respective roles in it. For example, the couple can decide on the rights of the visiting parent or the minimum standard of a second home before determining which parent will get custody or stay in the original home. This gives each partner a powerful incentive to negotiate a fair agreement.

Central to the success of this approach is the importance of not giving in to pressure, of a negative kind ('I'm going to walk out of here unless you make up your mind soon') or a positive kind ('Come on, don't you trust me or something?'). The only effective response to pressure is to invite the other party to restate their reasoning, to remind them of the mutually agreed objective criteria and to refuse to yield except on the basis of those criteria. Thus you remain calm, open to reason, objective and in a morally stronger position. This is a particularly effective strategy for those who are easily pressured. As the Harvard group points out, this is a case of right making might.

Questions and Answers

The ability to negotiate, to get what you want without engaging in destructive conflict, is an essential part of being effective at work and in your personal relationships. On the basis of two decades of experience in negotiating domestic, business and international conflicts, Roger Fisher, William Ury and Bruce Patton of the Harvard Negotiation Project have developed a set of principles that maximises the chance of making workable agreements, even when the other party refuses to negotiate or persists in using aggressive or bullying tactics.

The first task, according to the Harvard group, is to know your BATNA — your Best Alternative To a Negotiated Agreement. That is the standard against which any agreement should be measured and the only standard that will protect you from accepting a very bad agreement or rejecting an agreement that it is in your interests to accept.

If you have not thought carefully about what to do if you fail to reach an agreement, the Harvard group says, you are negotiating in the dark. You may break off negotiation little realising that the less than perfect agreement on offer is the best you may get. Many couples who are separating, locked in dispute about how much time the children will spend with each of them, may decide to go to court, not fully appreciating the almost unimaginable stress of a contested custody dispute.

But the greater danger is to have developed no alternative to a negotiated agreement and, when under pressure, to feel that you have to come to agreement at all costs, even if it damages your interests. What the Harvard group discovered is that the more you have thought out what you will do if you cannot reach agreement, the more powerful you are in the negotiation. This is because the relative negotiating power of two parties depends on how attractive to each is the option of not reaching agreement.

Developing this best alternative takes time and effort. You have to generate a number of options, turn these into practical proposals and select the one that seems best. It is also important to know what the other person's best alternative is. That allows you to be realistic about what to expect from negotiation.

If, for example, your partner is having an affair that is currently meeting many of his or her emotional and sexual needs, then negotiating about how to improve the marriage is largely a waste of time. In other words, the partner has too good an alternative. The issue then is to consider what you can do to change that situation by using all the time, information, money, support and intelligence at your disposal to develop the best solution for you, your best alternative, which is independent of your partner's agreement. Paradoxically, the more confidently you can walk away from a negotiation that is becoming pointless, the more you can get it back on track and effect what happens.

Apart from developing the elements of good negotiation, the Harvard group also perfected specific techniques for dealing with a difficult negotiating partner. For example, if the other person asserts a strong and (in your view) unreasonable position, the temptation is to criticise his or her position. They will then be more likely to attack your position and soon you will find yourselves locked into a vicious circle of attack and defence, pushing and pulling.

To break out of this cycle, the first step is for you to stop pushing back. Refuse to react; do not reject their position or defend yours. Instead, treat their position as one possible option and ask them how it can resolve the problem in hand. Ask what they think would happen if their position was adopted, what effect it might have on them and on you.

Similarly, don't defend your own ideas. Instead, invite criticism and advice. Ask them how your proposal would affect them, what interests of theirs it would not meet. Use the resulting information to adapt your own proposal and make it more attractive to the other side. Ask them what they would do if they were in your position, helping them to understand your part of the problem and maybe inventing a solution that meets your concerns as well as their own.

Asking questions instead of making statements is a key skill. Statements invite resistance. Questions generate answers. Having asked an honest question, it is then important to wait for the answer. In fact, the Harvard group considers that some of the best negotiating happens when you are not talking and that silence is one of the best negotiating techniques, particularly in the face of an unreasonable attack. Silence tends to make people uncomfortable, particularly if they have doubts about the merits of something they have said. Silence allows them the opportunity to answer your question more fully or come up with a new suggestion.

It is also important to divide the negotiating time into a phase where all the options can be discussed fully and a phase when decisions and choices have to be made. The first phase allows both parties the freedom to explore all the options without the pressure of committing themselves. Each option can be re-drafted, adapted, improved and tailored to better meet each side's interests, until one best option emerges.

Then, when it comes to decision time, each side has only one choice to make: accept or reject the best of the options. They know exactly what is on offer and the process of choice does not get tangled up with the negotiation. But it is a good idea in any negotiation to put a little time and distance between the two phases. Thus, a good negotiator comes to the table with a credible reason for leaving the negotiation when he or she wants to ('I'd like a day to think about it'). This allows time to verify matters of fact and to check that you have not lost perspective ('Yes, it's a good bargain, but do I really want it?').

If you find that the other side is using tactics that you feel are illegitimate (such as personal abuse, deception, upping the ante just as you've reached agreement), it is not a good idea to attack them personally. Question the tactic, not their character ('This discussion is getting too heated. I can't function well when I feel rattled. Would you like a break? I need some time to think about what's happening').

Finally, you must decide if you want to use tactics that you would consider wrong if they were used against you. You need to go away from this agreement not just with a solution to a problem and an intact working relationship, but with your own self-esteem undamaged.

Many of these principles and tactics may appear obvious, but the Harvard group fully acknowledges that the more consistent these ideas are with commonsense and intuition, the better. The more people are aware of what aspects of their instinctive style are likely to be productive in negotiation, the more confidently they can stand firm in that style. The more aware they are of the less productive techniques, the more possibility there is to change them. It is not easy to change your style, but in a world where the ability to negotiate has become central to a good and happy life, that change is worth the effort.

Middle Age: Is It All Over or Just About to Begin?

You know you are middle-aged if you feel, with increasing frequency, that if only you could take two weeks off from your life, you could get 'back to normal'. This feeling arises from the conviction that somehow, in your case, a mistake has been made. Yes, you have turned forty. You have noticed the changes in your body. You have become aware, with a mixture of surprise and irritation, that people in their twenties and even in their thirties, treat you as part of the establishment, one of 'them'. But despite all evidence to the contrary, this is not how you feel inside. You want to say: 'Hey, guys, I'm one of you, not one of them. Inside, I'm the same as I always was.'

For those on the brink of middle age, their own ambivalence about getting older ('Is it all over or just about to begin?') is matched by the conflicting cultural images of middle age. Middle age is variously seen as a period of entrenchment, conservatism, duty and responsibility, or as a period of profound frustration, dissatisfaction, and even of flightiness. The concept of the mid-life crisis is secure in the public's affections, conjuring up, as it does, the delightful and dreaded prospect of a pillar of society leaving behind the partner, children and colleagues who loved him (or her), to take off in a fast car with an entirely unsuitable younger lover.

What does the psychological research say about middle age? First the good news. The middle-aged tend to see themselves as the decision-makers, the standard bearers of society. Most feel themselves to be in the prime of life and observe striking improvements in their judgment and use of experience. They know what they are good at and how best to achieve their goals. They feel more competent, more self-aware, more selective, more in control of their environment.

They are highly sensitive to their position within a complex environment: in relation to work, family and the wider community. Middle-aged people see themselves as the bridge between the younger and the older generations. They feel themselves caught in a mid-life squeeze between the demands of the young, bursting to get a foothold in the adult world, and the demands of the old, determined to keep their foothold in life. They see themselves reflected in both their adolescent children (what they once were) and in their ageing parents (what they might become). In their offspring, they re-experience their own potential and their own vulnerabilities. Having lived long enough to have made their own mistakes, they feel closer to and more forgiving of their own parents.

Perspective on time changes. Life is no longer experienced as time since birth, but as time left to live. Particularly in the case of men, the physical changes associated with middle age serve as the markers of middle age itself. They realise that the time left to them is finite: they will die, things will remain undone. This intimation of mortality seems to be qualitatively different at mid-life than it is at earlier stages of the life cycle — death now becomes a psychological reality. A man in one study described it thus: up until mid-life, life seems like an endless upward slope, with nothing but the distant horizon in view. Now there is the experience of reaching the top of the hill, with the end of the road in sight, still very far away, but death is there, observably present at the end of that road.

Perhaps the most interesting insights on middle age came from Daniel Levinson's research, although he studied a relatively small group of people and included no women. His findings suggest that middle age is ushered in by what he calls the mid-life transition, which happens at about age forty and lasts on average for five years. Around this time, people have the experience of arriving at a culmination, a turning point in their lives. The decisive event may be some success or failure, some movement backwards or forwards in any facet of the person's life:

promotions or disappointment at work, satisfactions or dissatisfactions in family life, personal illness, the death of a significant person, recognition or devaluation in the wider world. Whatever it is, in the person's mind it symbolises the outcome of all the striving of young adulthood and plays an important part in instigating the mid-life transition.

The mid-life transition is a period of major reappraisal of the choices that were made in young adulthood. This involves the person asking a series of questions about their present life, that is, the work and relationships in which they invest most of their time and energy. The basic question is: how satisfactory is my present life — how viable in the world, how suitable to myself? This prompts a more general reappraisal. What have I done with my life? What do I really get from and give to my partner, children, friends, work, community — and self? What is it I truly want from myself and others? What are my central values and how are they reflected in my life? What are my greatest talents and how am I using (or wasting) them? Are there some things not now in my life that I want to include and some things I want to leave behind when I die? What was the dream or vision I had for my life and what do I want from it now? What are the possibilities for change in myself and in my world? How can I build a better structure for the future?

As they attempt to reappraise their lives at mid-life, people often discover how much has been based on illusion, that is, that their long-held assumptions and beliefs about themselves and the world are not true. For example, there is a growing awareness of the limits of willpower and ego, that is, the belief that 'if I do this or achieve that, I will be happy'. Even if a person has been highly successful by mid-life, there is a questioning of the meaning and value of the success ('Who am I doing this for?'). The life structure may be workable in the world, but personally unsatisfactory if it does not allow the person to live out crucially important aspects of themselves.

In this re-evaluation of the choices made in young adulthood, it becomes clear that the choice of career, partner, lifestyle and so on inevitably reflected only some aspects of the self. Of necessity, other aspects had to be ignored, repressed or remain undiscovered. This 'unlived life' assumes a new urgency at mid-life. There is the growing awareness, in Truman Capote's great phrase, of 'other voices in other rooms'. If this 'unlived life' is not attended to, there is the danger of a withering of self, of living a life that is not connected to self.

Levinson found that the person at mid-life has to resolve four basic dilemmas in the personality in his search to discover and develop the unlived life. First, a new balance has to be found between the polarities of being young and being old. The middle-aged person has to find a new way to be young and an acceptable way to be old. While it may be necessary and even liberating to give up some of the aspects of being young — being junior, naive, insecure — we cannot ever afford to give up other aspects of youth — being energetic, open, lively, daring, full of hope. Similarly, it may be possible and liberating to take on some aspects of being old — having wisdom, judgment, self-awareness — but it is crucial to minimise the other aspects of being old — being dried out, stagnant, losing power.

In fact, the spectre of middle age is stagnation: a sense of not growing, of being static, stuck, bogged down in a life full of obligations and devoid of self-fulfilment, of living in the shadow of death. The task of middle age, according to the psychoanalyst Erik Erikson is to become a productive, contributing member of society, to assume responsibility for a new generation of adults, both inside and outside the family, to become a senior member of the adult world, to leave a legacy of some kind to the next generation. Paradoxically, to do that, the middle-aged person first has to have the capacity to personally experience stagnation, to resist the temptation to deny it. Only by recognising the vulnerability in self is the individual capable of a new wisdom, and an imaginative tolerance and compassion for others. The task of middle age is keep this older, wiser self connected to the youthful sources of energy, imagination and daring in the personality.

The second dilemma is finding a new balance between destructiveness and creativity. By mid-life, everybody has experienced human destructiveness. In the face of the hurt caused by self and others, the person has to give up the myth that life is simple and that that there are no unknown or dark forces in the personality. He or she has to come to terms with grief over lost opportunities, rage over betrayal by others and guilt over betrayal of self. Mid-life calls for a new relationship with this dark side — what Jung called 'the Shadow' — not a withdrawal from or denial of it. Only by feeling an acute sense of his or her own destructiveness will the middle-aged person feel an intense wish to create something, to bring something new into being, to affirm life.

Thirdly, mid-life demands a new balance of the 'masculine' and 'feminine' aspects of personality. For those who have concentrated on the more masculine aspects of their personality (doing, making, having, achieving, concern with strength and power, with thinking, as opposed to feeling), there is the need to attend to the more 'feminine' aspects (sensitivity, feeling, nurturing, an enabling rather than an assertive energy) and vice versa. The aim is to give the undeveloped side a larger and freer part in the new personality configuration. When the masculine and the feminine are less rigidly defined within the personality, they can be combined more creatively in work and in mid-life relationships.

Finally, in middle age a better balance has to be found between the needs for attachment and separateness, between the needs of self and the needs of others. In a paradoxical way, as the middle-aged person becomes more burdened by responsibilities, there is a corresponding need to turn inward, to become more engaged with the self. If successful, the self assumes an importance for the individual roughly equal to that of the external world. The result is that the person can draw more on internal resources and become less dependent on external standards. In short, he or she becomes more mature.

On the basis of his research on adult lives, Daniel Levinson came to the conclusion that everybody's life was a sequence of structure-building and structure-changing, or transitions. To form a life structure, we must make certain key choices, mainly with regard to love and work. This process takes between five and seven years, ten at most. Then the life structure, because it has necessarily involved compromises and choosing against some options, begins to feel less satisfying, and even frustrating.

A period of questioning begins. The primary tasks of every transitional period are to reappraise the existing structure, to explore possibilities for change in your life and yourself and to move forward to make new choices and commitments that will form the basis for the next period of life. Transitional periods normally last about five years. Thus, almost half our adult lives are spent in developmental transitions.

We know a period of transition is ending when the questioning loses its urgency. We have a sense that the struggle is over (at least for now) to improve work, marriages, to come to terms with ourselves. We have to decide 'This I will settle for'. One of the most significant transitions takes place at mid-life, sometime between age forty and forty-five. During this transition, the individual has to evaluate the choices made during early adulthood, to see what progress has been made and the gains and costs to oneself. What is the outcome of this reappraisal process during the midlife transition? In the group of men he studied, Levinson found five basic patterns.

Advancement within a stable life structure. The men in this group (about 55 per cent of the group) had established a stable and successful life structure by the time they were forty. They had 'come a long way'. Yet, the majority experienced their success as somehow flawed — 'good but not great'— not sustaining all the hopes they had. There was a nagging fear that they would not reach their potential, or — a terrifying thought — that the potential was never there. Some, after initial and early success, remained stuck in frustrating work situations, feeling humiliated, knowing they had no future in their job, doing work that had no importance to them or to the organisation. Even those who had reached the top of one hierarchy were asking themselves: 'Where do I go from here?' To advance to the next level, they had to show real creativity just at the time when they were becoming aware of the limitations of their previous work. Most of the men in this category devoted much time and energy to the reappraisal of the mid-life transition and finally, through a combination of inner readiness and external opportunity, were able to move on. One example of this kind of mid-life transition was a biologist who at forty was a tenured professor in a distinguished university. In his early thirties, he had made an important scientific discovery and entertained serious hopes of making a dramatic breakthrough in his field. However, by age forty he was beginning to question what he was doing professionally. He realised with a shock that he had been working for several years on a spin-off from the original discovery and that if he wanted an eminent career he would have to define a fundamental new problem and begin large-scale research. His uncertainty about what was the most promising new direction for his research grew into a minor crisis. For the first time he had serious doubts about his creative talent.

The professor was spending a lot of his time in administrative roles in the university, which was further deflecting him from his research and his creative inner core. He had always felt himself to be the 'low man on the totem pole' with his own parents, being far from first in their affections, and began to realise that this had made him vulnerable to the pressures of the university to 'do the right thing', be responsible, and thereby get approval. He was beaten to a significant honour by another colleague and it became clear to him that he was not 'in the first rank'. He began to question the meaning and social value of his work, wondering what difference it would make in the longterm, and he often felt pessimistic and despairing. At the same time, the professor felt ashamed about what he regarded as his childish need to be always first, to need external kudos to make him feel good about himself as a man. Through long, intimate talks with colleagues he began to realise that many of his peers, even more successful than him, were plagued by similar feelings of disappointment and uncertainty. He started to invest more time in his relationship with his wife and young son.

By age forty-six, the professor was still struggling with some of the contradictions in his life and had not found any one thing to replace the dream of success which had given direction to his early adult life. But he had clarified the problem and had begun to define a life structure for middle adulthood. Satisfied that he had made a significant contribution to the university in his administrative roles, he relinquished those duties and began a large project in his new research field. He attracted many talented students to his laboratory and began to enjoy very much his role as a mentor. The most striking change was his greatly decreased need for recognition and his increased ability to gain intrinsic satisfaction from his work and his contribution to worthwhile social causes. He accepted himself as a middle-aged man of considerable achievements, experience and integrity — and of serious shortcomings. He had attained a sense of inner well-being.

Serious failure or decline within a stable life structure. The second group (about 20 per cent) knew they were doing badly and that their prospects were limited even before they reached mid-life. Only then, however, did they face the bleak reality and begin to consider other possibilities for their lives. They had to decide what to do with their lives now that they knew they could not become a man of a certain standing, a senior member in their world of work, a successful husband and father. Some never recovered from the crushing blow to their self-esteem and suffered a decline from which there was no escape. One executive, for example, had become an alcoholic in his thirties and had been moved to a 'non-position' in the company. By forty, his marriage had broken up and he was in serious ill-health. Others, after a prolonged and painful mid-life transition, were able to find new goals, new aspects of the self to be developed. Their failure shook them out of a rut and freed them from what were often unrealistic aspirations. They did not give up altogether on the idea of advancement, but defined success more broadly. For example, one middle-manager, having suffered miserably in a company where he was regarded as a failure, eventually left to start his own company as a consultant. He was then able to use his technical talents while avoiding the stresses of managerial authority and rivalry.

Breaking out. The third group (about 13 per cent) had established a stable life structure early in life but by mid-life their choices had become unbearable and so they 'broke out'. This usually involved a major change, such as a divorce or a radical job change. For the next few years, they made a concerted effort to make a new life which was more in accord with their values and aspirations. However, the process was very stressful. Because of commitments made earlier, they often could not devote themselves fully to their new activities. The new commitments quickly came under review as they entered further into their mid-life review and they were often faced with the possibility that these too had crucial flaws. Sometimes these men went through a series of painful changes over a period of twelve to fifteen years, but, for some the struggle ultimately resulted in a richer and better life.

One example of this pattern was a general manager of a company, who had divorced his wife and remarried and started a new family. He was promoted in the company but under a boss with whom he did not get on. He was tired of the relentless competition in his work, but afraid of giving up his aggressive striving. The flaws in his second marriage were becoming evident and these were exacerbated by a series of crises in his first family. His children from that marriage were beginning to experience serious problems and his second wife was thinking that she had married a family rather than an individual. He decided to put his family relationships more at the centre of his life and left his job. He was not sure what precisely he would do, but he planned to open a small business, run an antique shop with his wife and involve himself in teaching and consultative work. He eagerly looked forward to the changes in his life. His children's problems had abated and they were now settling down. The period of chaos was over and he was confident that he had found a new way of relating to his work and his family.

Advancement which produced a change in life structure. The fourth group (a very small number) experienced such dramatic success in their late thirties that it effectively had taken them out of their old life structure and catapulted them into a new one. This proved a mixed blessing and much of their mid-life transition was taken up with coping with the effects on their personal life of getting more than they had bargained for in the way of success. Like those who broke out, this group too found it difficult to create a new life structure at the very time they also were reappraising the mid-life transition.

One man, for example, had been unexpectedly promoted, but he had developed an ulcer and felt isolated and lonely in his new position. At the same time, a company reorganisation resulted in him getting a lateral shift to a position of less responsibility which he experienced as a great humiliation. Though he felt like leaving the firm, he eventually decided to stay. He had given up all pretence of interest in the competitive rivalries within the company and in further advancement. However he felt more secure in the environment he knew best. He had got through his crises only with the help of his family and now felt much closer to them and was learning to enjoy the pleasures of time with them. As he became more skilled in balancing his need for intimacy and solitude, he was emerging into middle age with a fuller life than he had had before.

Unstable life structure. The fifth group (again a very small number) were men who had been unable to form a stable life structure in early adulthood. They had experienced frequent changes in jobs, partners, homes, at a time when others were establishing stable lives. They were uniformly unable to cope with the tasks of the mid-life transition. One man, for example, had moved from teaching to educational administration, but was content in neither profession. He felt that he had made a series of compromises in work, marriage and other aspects of his life and now had a meagre basis on which to build for the future. Another who had hoped to become a novelist, lived a chaotic life, occasionally writing novels and film scripts, without a stable, intimate relationship.

Whatever the pattern, the crucial aspect of the mid-life transition is the process of appraisal: new choices have to be made that will give direction to life in the middle years. A person's life in the late forties, to the outsider, may look the same as life a decade earlier, but there are subtle but significant differences. You may be married to the same person, but the character of the relationship has altered appreciably for better or for worse. You may be in the same job, but you may be now just marking time before retirement or be more creatively engaged than ever in your work. You may have changed many aspects of your life, or very few. What matters is whether or not you have managed to imbue your life with a sense of inner excitement, a sense that you are taking a new step in psychological development, becoming more fully and uniquely yourself. That is what ultimately will determine the quality of your ageing.

Relationships

Unblocking the Prize of Real Intimacy

Falling in love, Freud observed, is not so much about finding a new love as refinding an old one, our intimate adult attachments being the ultimate development of the original parent-child relationship. It is from our parents that we learn the first lesson in love. We learn from others too, over time. But the deeper and more intimate the later relationship is, the more it involves rediscovering and remoulding our very earliest experiences of love and attachment. In adult intimacy we have a second chance at love, an opportunity to finish the unfinished business of childhood.

An increase in intimacy and interdependence in adult relationships is almost always accompanied by a sense of excitement, danger and risk because we find ourselves acting out of unconscious patterns that we can neither fully understand nor control. It is as if we cannot move on in an intimate relationship until the unfinished business of childhood is allowed enter the adult arena and we confront again the old fears of childhood.

There is no love without longing. Longing marks the birth of love. If a child experiences severe and frequent disappointment, that longing for intimacy is shut down. As adults we move deeper into an intimate relationship, that longing is re-experienced, with all its attendant memories of risk and disappointment. Once again, unconsciously, that longing may be extinguished. Consequently, we may deny our need for support and intimacy.

We may project an independent and strong exterior but remain deeply dependent at an unconscious level — the more typically male pattern. Or we may cope by rigidly and unconsciously repeating an infantile dependency, demanding immediate satisfaction of our needs, unable to tolerate frustration — the more typically female pattern. If we adopt either of these extremes, we will remain deeply ambivalent about dependency, with recurring patterns of approach-withdraw or dependence-independence characterising our adult intimate relationships.

Studies have identified six blocks to intimacy. People are afraid that their shortcomings and faults will be exposed in an intimate relationship; that if they allow themselves to become close, they will be abandoned; that information they disclose will later be used to attack them; that their own destructive impulses will be aroused if they let themselves go and express hidden feelings; that they will lose control if they deepen the relationship; that they will be swamped, taken over and lose their identity and individuality to their partner. One or other of these fears is almost invariably at the root of the apparently irrational and recurring conflicts experienced by couples as they move further into an intimate relationship. If these conflicts are confronted, the relationship develops and the old childhood hurt heals. If they are not, there is personal stagnation and the couple grow apart.

These fears, of course, have real origins, even if in rational terms they no longer have any justification in the context of our adult lives. The fears arise from early negative experiences with our parents, when we were intensely dependent on them for our very survival. We could not leave when they caused us fear or pain; in fact, we could not even articulate the feelings of power-lessness that became synonymous with ourselves. We sometimes had to make awful psychological compromises. If children experience constant frustration, punishment and threats of being cut off from love, the feelings of rage and fear which result are so overwhelming that the only solution is to repress — to split-off or deny — your own need for nurturance and comfort. You reduce the pain by pretending to yourself and to everyone else that you are invulnerable and independent; that you cannot be hurt any more. The price you pay is that your normal devel-opment, your capacity for intimacy, nurturance and interdependence, becomes frozen.

As adults, we bring all these frustrated, repressed emotional needs to our partners and this time we hope they will be met.

The trouble is that the repressed, split-off bits of ourselves have been in psychological cold storage since childhood. They have not grown up or developed. The repressed anger that finally emerges in adult intimate relationships has a toddler temper-tantrum feel to it. Fears of abandonment can rush back, reducing an otherwise competent adult to childish pleading and begging.

Sometimes, the split-off dependency needs are so intense and hidden that, no matter what the partner does, it cannot meet the depth of infantile longing to be taken care of. We search for signs that our partner is failing us, as *we* were failed before. We may distort reality, paying attention only to the responses that fit the childhood expectations of frustration and deprivation. We may even strike pre-emptively, protecting ourselves from even the possibility of disappointment by behaving in such a way that the partner has to leave the relationship, thus reinforcing the fear of future rejection.

What kind of relationship can break such a negative cycle? We often think of a good relationship as being synonymous with harmony, with feelings of contentment and happiness. But a good relationship, whatever form it takes, must also allow us to become whole: to reclaim the repressed, split-off parts of ourselves, to relax our old fears, to re-experience the intense dependency and fears of early childhood. If these needs can be acknowledged by our partners, they are made less dangerous in our own eyes and we can learn to accept them. For many people with less than perfect childhoods, that self-acceptance cannot be accomplished without a lot of psychological pain and conflict in their relationships. The prize for being truly known and loved is real intimacy.

The Gateway to Deepening Intimacy

Anybody who has ever been in love knows that a relationship stands or falls on whether or not the two people involved can build an intimate partnership based on trust. The engine that drives the development of relationships is the growth of inter-dependence between the partners. Becoming dependent on another person is what we most long for — and most fear. We long for that secure feeling that we can reliably depend on another to be there for us, especially in times of need. Yet, we know that the more dependent we become, the more vulnerable we are to exploitation and rejection.

Where does trust fit into this? Trust seems to evolve as the relationship between a couple develops, that is, as they become more dependent on each other *and* they successfully deal with their concerns about their dependence. Such concerns help explain the particular issues that seem to surface in every rela-tionship at different stages: issues of attachment, risk-taking, reciprocity, fairness and making the relationship part of the self.

At the beginning, the issue of trust hardly arises. Love is blind. We are swept along in a flood of passion. There are intense displays of emotion. Trust at this stage is often just blind hope that the relationship is somehow 'destined'. This conveniently gets over the fact that there may be little in the way of hard evidence to show if it can actually survive.

After the first burst of passionate feeling, the lovers have to begin the task of gathering information about each other, the raw data of trust. The goal is to reduce uncertainty, to reach con-fident conclusions about the other's investment in the relation-ship. The partner's behaviour is anxiously scanned for signs of true attachment, and the most basic sign is predictability.

When a partner's behaviour is predictable, each positive interaction becomes a building block in the growth of trust, a first sign that the partner is a dependable person. But this is not enough. Soon, it becomes critical to find out if the partner is dependable, not just because he or she is a reliable person, but because he or she cares about you in a unique way. In other words, there must be a quality of exclusiveness in the way the partner responds to you. This is the beginning of attachment and the relationship moves into a new phase.

As the couple become more dependent on each other, sooner or later their rising hopes about the relationship create a need for further reassurance. At this point, the critical issue to be negotiated is risk-taking. Before each partner can move deeper into the relationship, they need a sign that the other is prepared to take a risk or is willing to make some sacrifice of their own self-interest. In other words, the partner must show not just that they can give and take, but that they are prepared to go the extra mile, to make themselves vulnerable by investing more. They have to do something that, on the face of it, is not immediately justified by the other partner's behaviour.

Once one partner takes such a risk, inevitably the issue of the other reciprocating arises. In a well-functioning relationship, the other partner will respond in kind. Trust will then grow in an upward, positive spiral. The partnership becomes characterised by deepening cycles of reciprocity. Often the first major crisis in a relationship will be precipitated when the partner who has taken the risk becomes anxious about the involvement of the other partner. In fact, the doubt that love is not fully reciprocated is probably the best single predictor of the break-up of a dating relationship. This, of course, assumes that the doubting partner is not so emotionally insecure and needy that he or she is too afraid to act on well-founded anxieties.

If both partners have taken a risk, the stakes are now correspondingly higher and issues of fairness and equality become very salient. Each partner tends to keep a tally of what they are giving and getting in the relationship within a short time-frame. But partners want evidence of a balanced give-and-take, not just for the sake of equity or justice, but as evidence that the other is investing important resources in the relationship, truly cares about them and is thus committed to the future of the relationship. As these issues are resolved, worries about the short-term balance of give-and-take subside. Each begins to feel that the other really cares and will be responsive to their needs in the long term.

The task now is to tolerate uncertainty such that each investment in the partner or the relationship does not need to be immediately reciprocated. If this issue is not resolved, then concerns about reciprocity and equity become chronic. Anxiety about ensuring that your own needs are met and that you will get back what you put into the relationship can be crippling. These problems feature strongly in many distressed marriages.

If the couple successfully negotiate all these issues, they move further into a commitment to each other. Their lives become more intertwined. They come to know and depend on each other in a greater number of ways and at deeper levels. Inevitably, feelings of ambivalence begin to surface in a new way. The issues to be resolved now go beyond day-to-day interactions. They arise from the need to become a unit. The partners want to be close, but also fear the risks of becoming a couple. They resent the demands of becoming dependent on each other. The fear of losing their own identity and autonomy forces them to ask: 'Is this the right relationship for me?'

The challenge now is to find ways of accommodating each other at the deepest level of self, of creating a special and unique bond that, at the same time, will further the interests of each of them. It becomes critically to feel that you are understood, accepted and supported as you increasingly reveal your deeper self. This will show not just that your partner cares about you, but will powerfully reinforce your own sense of self and identity, allowing you to take the risk of becoming a unit.

If these tasks are successfully negotiated, the couple begin to feel that they have created a special bond and a sense of control over their common destiny. Concerns about self-sacrifice subside, because to give to the relationship is not depleting. Rather, the relationship is now part of the self. This is the gateway to intimacy. It is at this stage that real trust is established, independent of love. In other words, though partners may love each other, unless the issues of trust have been resolved, the relationship will ultimately run into chronic barriers to deepening intimacy.

Handing Over the Controls

A sense of control over your life is a vital ingredient of psychological well-being. Control means having a reasonable capacity to influence events and people that are important to you. But it also means being able to change the self, so that it fits better with the world and accommodates things that cannot be changed. In other words, an acceptance of some limitations on our ability to control events is a necessary ingredient of well-being. A healthy sense of control is equivalent to feeling that you have done the best possible — and maybe the only possible — thing given external circumstances and your own capabilities.

This is the level of influence which makes people feel that their life and actions have meaning. It is experienced at that point in a relationship when each partner can willingly and with open eyes relinquish personal control and put their fate in the hands of the other. Some people are never able to do that. Because of their unhappy experiences of childhood dependency, when being in the hands of another may have been so aversive, they may be incapable of making an act of trust again. Or their self-esteem may be so low that they do not feel entitled to voice their legitimate doubts about an unreliable, uncaring partner who really does not merit their trust. Either way, such individuals cannot trust that their needs will be met in the relationship. They put all their efforts into trying to control the partner in order to protect themselves. Control in this narrow sense becomes a substitute for trust.

Many distressed couples are caught up in such negative cycles. They try to achieve a desperately needed sense of security and worth by dominating every aspect of their lives together — money, decision-making, sex, socialising. The problem with any kind of excessive control is that there can never be enough of it. The more authoritarian power we exercise, the more power we think is needed to protect what we already have. This is as true of controlling relationships as of authoritarian states. Constantly struggling to maintain control over themselves and the partner, there is little possibility of learning anything new because the oppressed partner is afraid to give them any feedback, about mistakes made or opportunities missed.

How does this start? At the beginning of a relationship, achieving a sense of personal control is appropriate and indeed vital. Just as an infant has to feel that it can 'control' the parent by signalling its needs and having those needs met, the new lover has to feel that he or she can influence the partner.

It is not enough for a partner to be responsive. The apparent intentions behind that response are what counts. Three types of motivation are possible. First, the partner's responsiveness may be purely a selfish attempt to get something extrinsic (e.g. 'she is nice to me only because of my money' or 'he is being considerate because he likes being associated with an important person'). Second, the partner may be motivated by what the other is capable of offering as a person ('he is being attentive to me because he finds me so sexually attractive' or 'she cares about me because she needs the kind of support I can offer'). What we really desire is a third kind of motivation, where the partner is responding out of an intrinsic attachment — for no other reason but love.

Trust grows from the feeling that you are cared for unconditionally. It is not possible to risk relinquishing personal control over your destiny until you have that feeling. This is the stage when partners start talking of 'us' and 'our love' rather than 'me' and 'my love'. It is the stage when friends and family may begin to feel slightly excluded, slightly irritated. But for the couple it represents a turning point where the boundaries between self-interest and the individual partner's interest become blurred, when they experience a true sense of union for the first time. The relationship is valued over and above what the partner can offer. Of course, it is important to value the qualities which the partner brings to the relationship, and the other's support and praise further promote feelings of love, trust and satisfaction.

Some individuals cannot move beyond the first two kinds of motivation, that is, from calculating their own commitment in terms of what they hope to get from the partner in the way of direct benefits. If they occasionally take a risk and make themselves vulnerable by giving more, they are immediately overwhelmed by feelings of anxiety and rage that their gesture will not be reciprocated. Each time they make an act of trust, they are beset by the fear that they will be disappointed, as perhaps they were in an earlier relationship.

They may suffer such chronic insecurity about their needs being met that they will not even make these needs known. No amount of good experience or reassurance can allay their concerns. They are afraid that they will literally give themselves away. Because they cannot take the risk of relinquishing control over their own interests, they are doomed to see themselves as forever separate from the relationship and they experience extreme loneliness. They cannot reach that stage of trust where to give to the relationship is not really to give anything away if the partners are a unit. The paradox is that it is only by taking such risks and by relinquishing personal control that partners can achieve a very different kind of control, that is feeling they can fundamentally influence and determine the relationship itself.

Honesty and creativity in dealing with conflict are important in building trust and in dispensing with excessive or one-sided control. We know from research on creativity that what is required is a tolerance for ambiguity, an interest in exploring problems, rather than in finding quick-fix solutions, a willingness to suspend dominant or familiar structures of thought or ways of doing things, even though they may have worked in the past. In other words, creativity and problem-solving mean a relaxation of control.

It is not unusual for a partner in a very distressed marriage to report that he or she buried serious doubts about a partner and about the relationship at critical points because they were afraid that to air them would lead to conflict or rejection. Couples who confront the problems facing them at every stage get better at finding solutions, feel better about the solutions they come up with, and develop a better understanding of each other. The inevitable frustrations can be borne because they are perceived as having a purpose, as leading somewhere. They are part of the process of building the best possible — and perhaps the only possible — relationship between two unique individuals.

When Some are More Equal than Others

Most people now agree that intimate relationships between men and women should be equal. Yet while modern marriages — what we now call partnerships — are more equal than they used to be, the ideal of true equality remains elusive. Almost all studies still report that the reality very often belies the rhetoric. Most marriages remain hierarchical, with one partner (predominantly the male) more powerful than the other. A significant number of marriages still follow the traditional pattern of male provider/head of household, with a female fulfilling the complementary role of household manager and full-time mother. However, the more common pattern is a variation of that. The couple believe in and aspire to equality, in the notion of 'separate but equal' spheres of influence. The woman may work outside the home to help make ends meet, the man may help with the children, but the real responsibilities remain clearly differentiated into male earning-capacity and female caretaking. Each partner believes that the power in the marriage is distributed equally between them.

Alas, however, almost all the studies on such 'separate but equal' arrangements suggest that these partners do not really share equal power. The power relation is analogous to that between a senior and a junior partner in a company. The man has a veto power in a way that the woman does not. Theoretically, caretaking should be as elevated and as important as earning. In reality, as study after study shows, the person who earns the money gets to make all the rules, or at least those key rules which tend to be the focus of dispute between the couple. The power to make decisions correlates with income: the person who makes more money has more decision-making power, and the greater the distance between the incomes of the partners, the greater the control the high earner has. Even the woman who manages the household budget acts more as an agent of the family, like an accountant, rather than as a chief executive.

The linchpin of marital inequality is what Pepper Schwartz, a leading American sociologist, on the basis of twenty-five years research on couples, calls the 'provider complex'; that is, a combination of roles that gives the man the responsibility for financially supporting the family's lifestyle, and the woman all the auxiliary duties that allow a man to devote himself to his work. Clearly, the provider complex derives from the unequal position of men and women in the workforce. Men can command higher salaries and usually have better promotional prospects than women. But it is also related to expectations. The present situation may suit men, but women too are complicit in supporting this arrangement. Not only do many women choose to care for their children full-time, but in planning their careers they very often do not consider whether the job of their choice will support a family. In other words, women typically do not set out to become the main breadwinner, as men do.

Given these economic and psychological forces, it is not surprising that once children arrive, couples decide to revert to the 'separate spheres' pattern. Advocates of 'the new household economics', like Nobel Prize winner Gary Becker, believe that this pattern of 'separate but equal spheres' is the only reasonable goal. If the goal is efficiency, then it is clearly easier and less costly in terms of money, time, effort and psychological investment for women to take responsibility for child-rearing and men for providing. But what then of the possibility of ever changing those economic realities that make men's and women's positions so profoundly unequal?

Despite their initial commitment to sharing everything equally, once they become parents, many young couples end up reluctantly agreeing that 'separate but equal spheres' is the best and maybe the only arrangement, and hope they will deal with the consequences later. What are those consequences? Studies by Schwartz and other researchers suggest that it is almost inevitable that the male provider will eventually come to feel that his ability to keep the family going economically is dependent on the strength of the family support services. In other words, he will not expect to be burdened by domestic or child care duties that might interfere with his work commitments and he will feel that it is the woman's duty to protect him from such worries. Even when women work outside the family and feel that their earnings make a great contribution to the family income and believe their husbands fully appreciate this contribution, the research actually shows the women are misguided. To the provider, all other labour inside and outside the home, while vaguely welcomed, is seen as less important and onerous. The provider husband typically thinks his wife has an enviable life and has little real appreciation or even respect for what she does.

But the man's resentment at being in harness is gradually matched by the growing resentment of the woman at the amount of time and energy her husband devotes to his work. The more successful the husband becomes as a provider, the more the woman has to give up all previous demands for his time and cooperation. Ultimately their lack of communication so radically reduces interest in each other's worlds that respect, the bedrock of any relationship, is eroded. Traditional partners can offer each other token sympathy, but only shared experience (for example, experiencing the stress of having an idiot for a boss or shopping with a fractious toddler) can create empathy, that is, saying, with real feeling, 'I know exactly what you mean'.

Subscribing to 'separate spheres' simultaneously encourages and hides a hierarchy in the relationship. If a woman is in a 'junior partner' role, it seems churlish to ask her partner to cancel an important work arrangement when all she has to cancel is 'just' her arrangements. If she is taking time off to mind the children, it seems reasonable for her to tidy his clothes or for her to remember to collect the dry cleaning. These little services may start off as acts of care, but end up as acts connoting lesser status. One of the rewards of high status in any arena, work or home, is the ability to expect and ultimately compel that kind of service from others. After a while, there is a risk that such services come to be taken as a right or privilege, and recipients become irritable when they do not materialise as expected.

Schwartz found that, at the beginning of a relationship, a touch of inequality hardly seems to either partner like a threat to equal status, but conceding the husband's slightly senior status is the velvet noose for many marriages. Once established, such status differentials are difficult for both partners to reverse. The man will continue to verbally support the goal of equality, but only up to the point where it comes into conflict with his rights and privileges. Then, he will either explicitly assert that his rights are more important, or will plead for 'cooperation'. Either way, the woman will be expected to give in.

Schwartz's research shows that truly equal relationships have four characteristics. First, the partners have no more than a sixty-forty traditional split of household duties and child-rearing. Even caring for infant children involves a significant involvement of the father's time and responsibility. Second, each partner has equal influence over important and contentious decisions. Third, partners have equal control over the family economy and reasonably equal access to discretionary funds, and can undertake unsupervised private spending. Fourth, each partner's work is given equal weight in the couple's life plans. The person with the less lucrative or glamorous job is not, by definition, 'on call' to do most of the housework or child care. Money, influence, decision-making, child care and home-making are all shared equally; there is no hidden hierarchy.

What motivated these couples to make the extra effort to create and maintain equality was the promise of a deep and lasting friendship with each other. The reason they wanted to share all aspects of their lives was not as some book-keeping exercise of 'fair-shares' or some purely ideological commitment to equality. It was because, having observed their parents' and friends' marriages, or having themselves experienced unsatisfactory relationships, they wanted to avoid the pitfalls of the 'separate spheres' where each partner's day-to-day experience is so alien to the other that they become an increasingly irrelevant audience for each other. In more traditional marriages, the yardstick of marital communication — 'How was your day?' often comes to mean 'I'm just being polite. Just give me the bare outline'. Eyes glaze over halfway through the story because there is too much detail. Each partner comes to realise that it would take too much time to get the other to that point where the information about how the day really was would make sense or be compelling. The man chafes at the domestic trivia. The woman is bored by remote office politics.

Couples who were deeply committed to equality often decided to put the marriage and their children above economic success. Many of the partners — men as well as women — had decided to forego promotion or higher salaries if the cost was moving the family to a new area, longer hours, or more work-related travel. These couples had to fly in the face of the conventional wisdom — that equality is an inefficient, slow and messy business. Sharing tasks equally means that the person who is best at one job (making money or caretaking) has to waste their time doing other duties which they may not like or be good at. From the theoretical perspective of Becker's 'new household economics', equity that is each partner giving fairly but in different coin may seem more reasonable.

But equity is more elusive than equality and much harder to measure. Is attending the Parent Teacher Association equal (in importance and in personal effort on behalf of the family) to going to a conference in connection with work?

While such couples did not want to operate an exact accounting system of who does what household and child care duties, they realised that without equality (i.e. sharing tasks), it was too easy to slip into the traditional separate spheres with all their attendant status problems. Hence, they agreed that both would have significant involvement in all aspects of household management and their children's lives. More significantly, they shared not just duties but executive responsibility. In other words, both partners were also responsible for planning how these duties were to be done and by whom, for remembering important appointments and for initiating discussions about domestic and child problems.

Most crucially, they had come to realise that symbolic lapses were important. It really mattered that both partners did their fair share of laundry and school collections. They were able to make the necessary sacrifices because of their primary commitment to their relationship and family life. In effect, they had reversed the usual trade-off of time away from family, in return for income and career success.

Schwartz concluded that, if her study found anything at all, it was that allowing the provider role to dominate family organisation makes it impossible to have equality, companionship, paternal investment, and the kind of deeper friendship and respect that women and men say they want.

Sex Among Equals: Where's the Fun?

In the search for truly equal relationships between men and women, sex itself may be the last frontier. While feminists have engaged in the politics of reproduction and have championed the female orgasm, there has been relative silence on the matter of sexual desire. What is the relationship of sexual desire to troublesome notions of dominance and submission and the traditional roles assigned to each sex? In fact, there is a great resistance to such a debate, with men in particular fearing that any tinkering with sexual behaviour and roles will end up deconstructing gender itself, turning men into women and women into men.

Nowhere is the relationship between men and women more clearly defined than in their sexual relations. In the wake of the sexual revolution, our notions of eroticism remain stubbornly attached to the idea of male leadership in bed. Research has shown, for example, that when married couples disagree about sex, men's wishes are more likely to prevail. More particularly, the right to initiate sex and the right to refuse it are still firmly assigned to men and women respectively. Nowadays, women are more active, experimental and even daring in their sexual relationships. Men like this. They even like the novelty of women occasionally initiating sex with them. But they do not, apparently, want them to do this routinely.

When women ask for sex more than their male partners do, couples report greater conflict about their sex life and less satisfaction. In this situation, the women too are disappointed. They do not want to be in the role of initiating sex, any more than their partners want them to be. In fact, many women report that they sometimes repress their own desires so as not to pressure their male partner. Sometimes they are reluctant to make sexual advances because they feel that their partners are off-form, vulnerable, insecure. But at other times, it is because they are unsure if their attempt to initiate sex will fall into the category of the occasional permissible novelty, or as a 'take over' from the traditional male role as sexual leader. If men want to be in charge of 'desiring', then women want to be in the role of 'the desired'. In return for her more passive role in sex, the woman is granted 'permission', albeit reluctantly, occasionally to refuse sex. However, when men refuse sex, women often feel angry.

Hierarchy itself can be erotic. The fantasy of male leadership and control is, it seems, inherently erotic. Female sexual fantasy is still often anchored in the desire to be 'swept away' by a lover who is dominant, confident and knows what he is doing. The woman is also aroused by the fact that the man's desire for her momentarily changes the power relation between them. She controls the controller. Similarly, the man is aroused by the woman's surrender. His desire is energised by the idea of 'taking' a woman, by the display of his own physical power and strength, by his ability to act decisively, and by his skill in eliciting a deeply erotic response from his partner. Women can be irreverent or seductive, but their erotic role is ultimately to be accessible and deeply responsive. It is no linguistic accident that many slang expressions of 'being got the better of' are sexual and refer specifically to the woman's role in sex.

For many men and women who are publicly committed to the idea of sexual equality, such erotic fantasies remain a lingering embarrassment. But can we have equality in the cold light of day and archaic sexual dramas of dominance-submission in the dark? What happens when couples strive to have truly equal relationships inside and outside the bedroom? What happens to sex when hierarchy, with its attendant notions of male leadership, disappears from a relationship?

On the basis of her studies of couples, Pepper Schwartz suggests that those couples committed to cultivating a deep and equal friendship, and to relinquishing traditional gender roles, incur costs. For certain couples there developed something akin to an incest taboo. There was such closeness and similarity that sex came to seem almost incestuous, or at the very least lacking a certain erotic charge.

In some respects, the major erotic pitfall for such couples was one that afflicted all long-term relationships — only worse. Traditional eroticism is anchored in difference. The more men and women keep themselves separate, living lives that are strange to the other, the more traditionally 'masculine' and 'feminine' they seem to each other. The less each 'knows' the other, the more mystery there is. This kind of mysteriousness can be powerfully erotic.

For couples who shared all aspects of their lives, passion was often compromised by increasing familiarity, by allowing the sexual relationship to be taken for granted and pushed to the end of their agenda. Domesticity, especially when it is shared, can extinguish sexual passion. Passion is evoked by the desire for connection, the urge to bridge some real or symbolic gulf between the partners. The problem of equal sharing is that it can appear that there are no more gulfs to cross, no differences to excite. Not only do conversations about the job and the children and household chores have a way of spilling over into what should be sexual conversation, but if one partner feels the other knows them really well, it becomes difficult to make the essential transformation from the everyday self to the erotic self.

A second problem can arise from the very security and contentment of the relationship. Sexual passion often is the positive by-product of tension, conflict or insecurity. Paradoxically, the more secure the relationship, the more elusive the passion. The drive for understanding and acceptance creates harmony and balance. Sexual attraction remains, but the dangerousness, novelty and risk can go, and sex can become too comfortable and unexciting.

The passion of equals, not predicated on hierarchy, has to find another fuel. Some of the couples in Schwartz's study had worked out successful ways to confront the challenge. Being exceptionally intimate, each partner had to fight the temptation to be consistent with the person the other knew them to be. Those who succeeded had become adept at granting the partner 'permission' to transform their identity during sex, such that they could escape the confines of everyday life. Sexual gameplaying, often involving fantasies of dominance-submission, were explored, in the secure knowledge that identities in bed would not spill over into identities outside the bedroom. Traditional erotic imagery, positions and role-playing were not off limits, but they were included in a more playful, experimental and deliberate way. And, most importantly, such sexual play had no implications as to who would later do the dishes, put out the rubbish or bring home the bigger pay cheque.

In addition, both partners made sure that sex actually happened, that it happened the way each person needed it, and that it had not fallen into a rote pattern. The person with the greater sexual appetite, not always the man, had the greater responsibility to make sex happen. The erotic and intimate payoff emanated from the knowledge that each partner had seen unexpected aspects of the other. Only that person knew what the other was capable of. One advantage was that the problem of sexual reciprocity in traditional relationships was avoided. For example, in more traditional couples, because initiating sex is the male privilege (and duty), women find themselves responding to the man's desire, rather than to their own, and are sometimes frustrated when they want sex. This problem of mistiming may account for the finding in one study that most women admitted that they had faked orgasm at some time in their marriages and nearly half still continue to do so.

The 'equal' couples also explored the possibility of eroticising similarities. They may be the pioneers. For example, men are only just beginning to experience the novelty of being sexually attracted to powerful women whom they identify as being like themselves. One study suggests that successful, high-earning women try to be sexually available and responsive to their partners to an exceptional degree, almost as a way of rebalancing the power relations in the marriage.

'Equal' couples worked to retain a separate identity as lovers, that is, separate from their role as domestic partners and parents. They often invented a special sexual reality which allowed them to escape the confines of ordinary, everyday life. For example, they set up contexts where work and domestic identities were forbidden, mundane conversations avoided, and parental and economic concerns postponed. Physical appearance was taken seriously. They continuously tried to stretch the boundaries of sexual game-playing, particularly games of dominance-submission where the roles were regularly swapped.

Whatever the potential difficulties in equal relationships, it is well to remember that there are also sexual failures in more traditional relationships. For example, because 'traditional' couples do not communicate so openly and deeply, they may not be sufficiently intimate with each other to risk revealing their exact sexual desires or needs. Most importantly, there may be failures of reciprocity. In general, women in such relationships are expected to give more, and men are less likely to touch, massage or perform particular sexual acts than they receive from their female partners. In fact, Schwartz identified reciprocity in bed as one of the signal elements of equality in marriage.

Despite what Schwartz called the 'passion problem' in a sexual democracy, almost all the couples felt that their romantic lives were exceptional. Certainly, the couples who had achieved equality described lives of impressive mutual commitment and affection. Both parents invested significant time and energy in the welfare of their children. The considerable time they spent together resulted in a deep intuitive understanding of each other. They were in stark contrast to the more traditional couples where women complained of being emotionally neglected and men were often bored and angry that their marriage was reduced to recriminations from their wives punishing them for their emotional deficits.

This growing body of research is heartening, suggesting that the elusive goal of true equality is possible, but only by departing radically from traditional marital patterns and by a willingness to pay a certain price. The question is: are we ready for this particular revolution?

Do You Want to Talk About It?

Picture the scene. The woman feels dissatisfied, unhappy; she wants something from her partner that she's not getting. It could be more discussion, better sex, help with the children or the house. She conveys this to him, directly and indirectly. She sighs, she hints, she argues, she says 'we must talk'. The man feels crowded, under pressure. He says he sees no need to talk about whatever it is that is bothering her or, more likely, he says he does not feel like talking now. She says he never feels like talking about it. How much longer does she have to wait? He says he does not know what she is talking about: they're talking now, aren't they? What more does she want?

She feels hurt, ignored. She intensifies the pressure to deal with the problem. He withdraws further, lapsing into a tense silence. She feels shut out. She becomes agitated and comes back at him with a more urgent demand to talk. He retreats even further — emotionally, by ignoring her, or physically, by leaving the room or the house. She becomes even more upset, bursting into tears or into a torrent of criticism of him. Each blames the other for starting the row. Both end up feeling that the other is impossible. She says she has to put all this pressure on him because he withdraws from her and will not deal with the problem. He says he withdraws because of all the pressure she puts on him. Each feels put-upon and powerless to stop this destructive pattern of dealing with each other.

Over and over again, researchers have shown the prevalence, especially in unhappy marriages, of interaction patterns such as the one described above. What is going on during this demand/withdraw pattern? How is it understood by men and by women? How can it be stopped?

Two issues have been found to underlie this pattern. First, the most significant predictor is the difference in the degree of intimacy and independence desired by each of the partners in a relationship. In most relationships, women want more intimacy and try to achieve it by demanding something from their partners. Men, on the other hand, want more independence in the relationship and seek it by withdrawing. This will normally be contained within the sporadic crossfire of gender relations.

However, if the differences in desired intimacy and independence are great, full-scale war breaks out. Then the demand/withdraw pattern will characterise nearly every interaction, the relationship will be distressed and neither partner will achieve their goals. Of course, the fatal attraction is between partners, one of whom is highly dependent and clingy, the other remote, rigid and reserved.

The second issue is how each partner handles conflict. Both find conflict upsetting and stressful, but perhaps the most surprising finding is that it is women, rather than men, who feel more at home having an argument in an intimate relationship. Women, it seems, are the real warriors of love. Because they so passionately believe in the power of talk, they are convinced that every conflict can be resolved, if only they can get their partners to understand their point of view. Thus, in situations of conflict they redouble their efforts to get closer. In their efforts to achieve intimacy, women pull out all the expressive stops. Anger can make a women feel independent and assertive. What, in the meantime, is happening to her partner?

Anger, it seems, is making him feel helpless and out of control. Men may become anxious because they feel they lack the skills to deal with the conflict. Or it may be that because of their higher levels of aggression, men feel responsible for exercising control in a situation of mounting conflict and are anxious because they fear they may lose control. The more difficulty a man has asserting himself appropriately, the more distressed the relationship.

Moreover, there is intriguing evidence that men's greater difficulty in dealing with conflict has at least a partly physiological basis. Men, it seems, are more physiologically reactive to negative emotional situations and take longer to return to resting, or pre-stressor, autonomic nervous systems levels than do women. Since emotional conflict is more physiologically costly and punishing for men, it follows that they will be more inclined to avoid it.

The problem with such a negative cycle of interaction is that it tends to assume a life of its own. Once the cycle has started, men and women are like partners in a mad dance; neither feels fully in control of their own behaviour. Given the self-perpetuating nature of such destructive cycles, men will continue to see withdrawal as their only way out of an argument or quarrel, and women to see pressure as the only possible response to the emotional withdrawal of their partners, unless at least one of the couple changes the steps of the dance.

The key is to begin to understand the issue that precipitates the cycle. For many couples, the reluctance of the man to acknowledge the legitimacy of the woman's dissatisfaction is what starts the cycle. This in turn is due to men's reluctance to accept that feelings are data, irrespective of the merits of the case, as it were. If a woman is frustrated or deprived, this feeling will have to be dealt with, even if her partner truly believes she has no reason to be that way. Many rows could be short-circuited if the response to a complaint, from either partner, were along the lines of 'I accept that you feel that way; tell me more about it', rather than the defensive 'I do not accept that you feel that way.'

Women need to deal with the fact that men find intense interpersonal conflict disabling and to find ways to help men to open up, rather than to pressure them to the point of withdrawal. Both partners must understand the value of dealing with conflict in the early stages, when emotions are not yet running high. Couples should find ways to disengage from disagreements that are getting out of hand, to devise a mutually agreed, honourable way to make a short-term retreat. Finally, to prevent the retreat turning into a long-term avoidance of the source of the dispute, they need to agree to discuss the issue at a later, specific time.

Communication

Try this. Pretend you are asking your partner the following questions: 'What are you doing? Do you really want to watch the rest of that? Do you know what some thing like that costs?'

Ask the questions in three different ways. First, in a positive way, as if you anticipate an answer that will please you. Second, in a neutral way, as if just curious to know. Third, in a negative way, as if you are annoyed, suspicious and anticipating a reply that will antagonise you even further. Undoubtedly, you will find out for yourself what is already known from psychological research: that the actual word-content of a message conveys only a fraction of what we communicate. To get our meaning across, we all rely predominantly on non-verbal channels. It has been estimated that about 7 per cent of communication is achieved by the spoken message, 38 per cent by verbal expression (like tone of voice) and 55 per cent by facial expression.

Psychologists studying communication between spouses have discovered that there are intriguing differences between men and women, and between happy and unhappy couples. Two elements of good communication have been identified: sending clear messages and accurately deciphering messages received. It has been found that for a lot of couples, particularly unhappy ones, there is many a slip between the communicative intent (the message one spouse wanted to send) and the communicative impact (the message the other spouse actually received).

For example, unhappy couples frequently interpret communication from each other as being far more negative that it was actually intended to be — apparently due to their poor ability to decode each other's non-verbal cues. When there is ambiguity in a communication, men are much more likely to assign a negative interpretation, whereas women are likely to interpret it more positively than it actually was intended to be.

If you were to look at what couples actually say to each other, much of their communication would seem neutral. Couples rely on the accompanying non-verbal behaviour to convey the tone of the communication, particularly in the case of positive messages. Positive messages are conveyed, for example, by open and closed smiles and raised eyebrows. Negative messages are conveyed by frowns and eyebrow furrows. In addition, women tend to use more non-verbal behaviour and therefore to be better communicators than their husbands. They send more accurate, expressive messages, clearly differentiating by a range of non-verbal behaviour when they want to send positive, neutral or negative messages.

Husbands, on the other hand, use similar non-verbal behaviour for most messages, apparently placing great reliance on eyebrows; they raise and 'flash' their eyebrows whether they are sending positive or negative messages. Naturally, this often leaves their partners befuddled and obliges them to spend more time figuring out precisely how their husbands are feeling. Meanwhile men complain that they cannot understand why women ask so many questions about how they (the men) are feeling. More raised eyebrows.

Women are especially good at sending positive messages. However, it is the male partner's communication skill that makes the critical difference between happy and unhappy marriages. Research shows that husbands in happy marriages are better than those in unhappy marriages at sending accurate messages to their wives, particularly positive messages. Women in unhappy marriages complain about the lack of positive communication from their husbands: they want more affection, appreciation and attention. Unhappy marriages suffer from a lack of such positive behaviour, with husbands not succeeding in getting across the few positive messages they do attempt to send. Husbands in unhappy marriages are further handicapped by a tendency to rely primarily on their wives' facial expression when interpreting messages. The problem is that depending on facial expression is less effective than paying attention to tone of voice.

Sadly, couples in general seem to have no difficulty in getting across negative messages. But unhappy couples accompany their messages with much more negative non-verbal behaviour and tend to set each other off in negative cycles. Thus, a negative message from one spouse leads to an even more negative reaction from the other, and so on. Happy couples tend to deal with negative messages, such as criticism, in more constructive ways. They seem to frame or envelop any negative message they send or receive with positive feeling. It is as if their generally comfortable, happy feelings for each other 'leak' into their interactions, softening the impact of negative events. For unhappy couples, the opposite is true, with their resentment and unhappiness 'leaking' into every interaction, souring positive messages, intensifying negative messages and putting a negative bias on neutral messages.

Criticism kindly conveyed with a touch and a smile is saying: 'I don't like what you are doing, but I still like you.' Praise or thanks conveyed without smiling or holding the gaze is saying: 'I acknowledge what you did, but I do not care much about you.' Similarly, an angry exchange saying 'I don't care what you do anymore', accompanied by a frightened expression and clutching at your own body, is conveying a different message. It is saying 'Take pity on me. I need you.'

Learning how to communicate better has to start with an awareness of how we feel about ourselves and our partners. Very often we embody unconscious feelings in our posture, facial expression, gestures, or tone of voice. While our words may convey one message to our partner, our body language may be saying something contradictory.

Are couples aware of possible communication problems with each other? Do they usually assume that the message sent is always the one received? In general, couples seem to know when they have communicated well or badly. However, unhappy couples tend to have an unwarranted confidence in their communication skills, frequently assuming that they are correctly interpreting when in fact they are misunderstanding what the spouse is trying to communicate.

Couples who try to improve their communication almost always concentrate on their verbal interactions. Yet the evidence is that it is non-verbal communication which is decisive in determining the quality of a relationship. In therapy, the first step is often to help couples to become aware of the non-verbal dimension. Couples are encouraged to check with each other that what was actually said and intended by one was what the other heard. Research also highlights the need for men to become more aware of and skilled about communication, since it is the communication skills of men which discriminate best between happy and unhappy couples. In addition, such skills need to be taught at their place of close relationships, because while men may be good communicators in the context of work, they often lack the different skills needed for intimate communication.

Gay and Lesbian Relationships

'Ten years ago, we thought we knew everything about couples.' This was the opening statement of an address which for many delegates was the highlight of a 1995 international conference on personal relationships. The paper went on to document the proliferation of studies on gay and lesbian relationships over the past decade. The initial role was to identify the differences between gay and lesbian couples, on the one hand, and heterosexual couples on the other. In the process, however, the research throws new light on the differences between men and women — differences that in many cases transcend the issue of sexual orientation. More recent research has also succeeded in breaking away from the preoccupation with what 'causes' homosexuality and focusing instead on the whole people in gay and lesbian relationships — their needs, concerns, strengths and weaknesses.

Clearly, AIDS has overshadowed relationships in the gay community, but research shows that the search for commitment in intimate gay relationships happened before the AIDS crisis and probably has always been important for lesbians. Like heterosexual women, most lesbian women give priority to emotional characteristics when looking for a partner (the exceptions being what in the US are called 'lipstick lesbians', who seek out more conventional female beauty in their partners). Gay men, like heterosexual men, are more preoccupied with physical appearance. Lesbians are also much more wary of entering relationships with bisexual partners than are gay men, fearing that such women ultimately will disappear into the heterosexual community, leaving them feeling exploited and betrayed.

Because gay men (like men in general) are generally financially better off than lesbian women (like women in general), women's organisations have become very important focal points for lesbians to form political alliances and empower themselves. Lesbian relationships therefore tend to be heavily influenced by the political nature of the gay community in which they live.

A primary concern of lesbian relationships is achieving a working balance between the need for autonomy and the need for closeness. Because they are women, strong attachments are important. Because they are lesbians, forging a non-traditional image of strength and independence is also vital to these women's identities. With both partners having the same needs, many lesbian couples find it difficult to keep a balance between attachment and autonomy.

Too much focus on attachment leads to complaints of emotional suffocation, a drift towards fusion, feelings of panic about 'who's who here?', and sometimes to a break-up of the relationship. Too much focus on autonomy leads to complaints of the partner being too cold, too distant, not 'giving' to the relationship. Researchers had expected that lesbian relationships would be the most stable ones, approximating to stable marriages. Instead, they found a very high break-up rate among lesbians, perhaps because of the raised expectations they bring to their intimate relationships.

To what extent do gay and lesbian couples share the same communication patterns as heterosexual couples? To a remarkable degree it seems. We know, for example, that women in general tend to use conversation to establish intimacy and rapport, rather than simply to exchange information. While listening to another woman talking, women use a constant stream of encouraging sounds and speech ('I know, I know, M'mm, yes') to convey a feeling of sharing, solidarity and empathy. Men, on the other hand, tend to use conversation primarily as a way of conveying information. (e.g. Woman: I'd love if we talked more. Man: But what do you want to talk about?). Men also use more power tactics like interrupting the person speaking so they can hold the floor themselves.

In some ways, these gender differences are exaggerated in predictably opposite ways in gay and lesbian relationships. For example, gay men tend to give their partners fairly minimal conversational responses. Interactions tend to be punctuated by a lot of 'Ah, hahs' and 'Uh, huhs'. And, since each partner, following the typical male pattern, attempts to dominate what conversations they do have, the partners in gay couples tend to have the lowest rate of actually successful interruptions. It may often be a while before anyone gets to talk.

Lesbian couples, in contrast, tend to be vividly aware of power imbalances in conversations. They have the lowest rate of attempted interruptions, the fewest conversational challenges and the fewest arguments. Their conversations were punctuated by many 'What do you think?' probes. Literature from the world of work suggests that bosses do not like to give direct criticism to women employees because the women tend to take it personally (a view affirmed by women). Lesbian women also do not seem to like being challenged directly by their partners. They expect their relationship to run on a 'friendship' model.

Instead of fighting and conflict, they try to deal with issues through discussion. This strategy can create its own set of problems. Lesbian relationships tend to make every disagreement an 'issue', so much so that the very number of issues and the intensity of all the discussions become a burden. Lesbians want to avoid conflict because, like women in general, they have high expectations that their partner should know what they are thinking. Their feeling is that if they have to discuss it, it is too late.

This is in contrast to gay couples, who identify hardly any issues, preferring not to look at a potentially contentious question until it is seriously affecting their relationship. As a consequence, when they do deal with a problem, it is often when it already has got out of hand. The fights, as a result, are more intense. Gay men are more likely to challenge each other without listening to what the other is saying and they dislike compromise. They seem to accept that such conflict is inevitable, taking the view that that's what men do, and that things are bound to get rough now and again.

Gay men are also much more willing to confront issues of power imbalance and engage in power struggles about things that are important to them, like money. They believe in the privilege of money and the perks of being the provider in the relationship. In fact, the issue of who, if anybody, is the provider, is very contentious. Usually, the partner being provided for does not like being in this position and is the most likely to leave the relationship. In lesbian couples, neither partner wants to be in the role of provider, and the partner who makes the most money is the one most likely to leave.

For both gay and lesbian couples, as indeed for heterosexual couples, housework and the division of labour are big issues. Gay men, being generally better off, tend to solve the problem by hiring help. Housework is more stigmatised for women, being associated with traditional female oppression. Thus, lesbians do not like hiring other women to do their housework for them. They often solve the problem by having untidy houses. In fact, for lesbians, at least in the highly politicised gay communities in the United States, the whole notion of 'home' is often associated with oppression, whereas for gay men, with their different cultural baggage and higher incomes, homes are often showcases for their artistic and aesthetic sensibilities.

For both gay and lesbian couples, the issue of monogamy is central. In the 1980s, 97 per cent of gay men were non-monogamous. Now, 97 per cent are monogamous — a startling turnabout. Lesbians who break up, frequently do so because they fall in love with a friend. Since love and friendship are so tied up for them, it is easy to see how friendships can drift into love, disrupting not just their primary intimate relationship, but complicating the social network within which they socialise. Gay couples, on the other hand, tend to operate an informal 'incest taboo', rarely falling in love with close friends.

The more often that gay and lesbian couples are studied, the more difficult it will be to forget that they are real people, not cultural icons. They experience the same problems and failings as heterosexual couples: physical and verbal abuse, violence, and rape within their relationships. More so than heterosexual couples, however, they try to manage their relationships within an egalitarian framework. It is rare to find a gay or lesbian relationship where one partner is both sexually and socially dominant. In gay and lesbian relationships, more powerful partners seem to use less power tactics than their heterosexual counterparts. Both partners try to modify their gender style, as it were in the interests of a more equal power balance between them. Such couples are struggling with issues of equality in a way that will ultimately help us to separate the issue of gender and power in all intimate relationships.

When the Old Triangle goes Jingle Jangle

Nobody commits adultery anymore. They have affairs. The word 'affair' is cooler, less judgmental. But the breach of what is meant to be a sexually exclusive bond is rarely a cool issue. Surveys in the United States show that over three-quarters of all adults believe affairs to be always wrong, constituting a serious threat to marriage. Yet there are few subjects that fascinate people more. There is something about the inherently unstable triangle of the affair that deeply engages the human psyche.

Everybody has a theory about affairs. Some feminists argue that women have affairs to escape the unutterable loneliness of being married to men who do not love them or make them feel special. But what about the straying husbands? Men at fault again, I'm afraid. An insatiable desire for sex and power over women, irresponsibility and self-indulgence are the favoured explanations. There is, of course, some sleight of hand here. The affair is cast as a revolutionary act in the case of women, a shot across the bows in the war between the sexes. In the case of men, the affair is presented in somewhat less flattering terms, as a rather pathetic male ego trip.

Men, understandably, do not see it that way. They tend to cast the affair as an existential foray, an act of defiance against the iron destiny of fate and death, evoking the image of Hercules in domestic chains, the boyish, reckless warrior of love lurking inside every caring, providing husband.

Psychology and psychoanalysis, by and large, rise above the gender crossfire and treat the affair as something not quite for grown-ups. The affair is treated as a symptom of an individual's psychological frailties or of an ailing marriage.

For example, affairs may occur when one or both of the partners reaches an emotional 'glass ceiling'. They find themselves unable to break down the barriers to sexual or emotional intimacy with their partners. They start to feel bored, depressed, dissatisfied. Very often they lose all sexual desire for the partner. Unconsciously, this lack of desire may be covering up hostility towards the partner for 'keeping' them in the relationship, or for making emotional demands on them to which they cannot respond. Or the lack of desire may be a defence against their own fear that they are incapable of love, it being easier to admit to a lack of desire (which may not be their fault) than to an incapacity for love.

Affairs are a major diversion from this particular form of unhappiness. 'No-hope' relationships may be started with lovers who are unavailable in a long-term way because of family commitments, personality problems, or because they have a long history of other affairs. Thus, there is a built-in guarantee that the illicit relationship will never reach the stage of making real demands.

Then there are those people who emerge from childhood with a perilously heavy load of unresolved problems. They seem caught forever in the classic oedipal triangle of their original family — mother, father, child. As adults, they are drawn to the forbidden, to the legitimate sexual partner of another. They like to play the perfect 'other woman' or 'little husband'. The real or imagined jealousy of the rival is a major factor in the excitement of the affair, the expectation that this time, unlike in childhood, they will be powerful and seductive enough to oust the rival.

Carl Jung believed that affairs often happen in mid-life when individuals become aware of their 'complex' nature and long to express and unify the different facets of that nature. They feel confined by the 'simpler' nature of their spouse and decide to develop themselves, as it were, outside the marriage. Typically, the partner who had been valued for providing an island of stability at the end of adolescence may now appear to be the personification of dullness in mid-life. A husband who had been valued for his easy-going, non-demanding sexuality by a sexually inexperienced, shy young woman can come to be seen as too passive and lethargic later in the relationship. The restless partner may try to express this new side to themselves, the unlived part of themselves within their relationship, but find that the other partner is too settled, or threatened, to accommodate it.

This restlessness and desire to break loose very frequently occurs in those relationships in which the partners have fallen into playing a quasi parent-child role with each other. The wife may be kept in a childlike, dependent role by a very traditional husband. Or a controlling wife may infantilise her husband by allowing him or even covertly encouraging him to play the role of *enfant terrible*. Either partner may tire of their role and are most vulnerable to an affair if they meet somebody who recognises and admires the new side to themselves. If a hitherto dependent person discovers a powerful, assertive side to his or her personality, there is nothing quite as irresistible as a lover who recognises and affirms that new-found self.

Even the most stable of marriages can become vulnerable to the danger of an affair when events, such as an unexpected death of a family member, a major career disappointment, or even a big promotion, psychologically unsettles one of the partners, exposing a side of the self that cannot easily be accommodated by the other partner.

Of course, even the most settled and psychologically mature people occasionally fantasise about having an affair because most people long for erotic and romantic intensity in their lives. But it is difficult to keep passion, particularly sexual passion, alive in a long-term relationship. Sexual behaviour surveys show that sex with the same person over long periods tends to become less exciting. This loss of initial excitement may be compensated for by the increasing depth of the emotional relationship. But the desire for sexual excitement and novelty remains strong.

Romantic intensity is also difficult to sustain in the context of the relentless demands of domesticity. Romance thrives on novelty, secrecy, risk-taking, obstacles. The function of domestic life is precisely to reduce all these. Even the most committed partners dream of the bliss of an uncomplicated romantic liaison and occasionally despair of recapturing the intensity of falling in love, of going to meet the lover oblivious to everything except the anticipation of what it will be like to make love. They cannot bear the thought that they will never again love or be loved to distraction.

In this frame of mind, an affair can seem like a glorious respite from domesticity, from growing old and tired, from yourself. It can provide an unparalleled opportunity to trot out all your old lines. But an affair rarely solves your existential problems, or even your psychological ones, and, at worst, is a dangerous dalliance with very powerful feelings.

The End of the Affair

The discovery that a partner has been unfaithful is devastating. In Harold Pinter's play *Betrayal*, the action moves backwards, revealing the lies and deceptions that preceded the dissolution of the relationships between the husband, the wife and her lover. The discovery of an affair has the same effect. Given this new information about the partner, what now can be taken for granted? Was it an isolated incident? If not, what other affairs have occurred? If the partner lied about this incident, how can you now trust his or her answers to any further questions?

As the details of the affair emerge, everything that happened around that time has to be re-examined. What had been safely consigned to the past as a shared life, a communality of experience, has to be summoned back, unravelled. Like a split-screen, the affair is imagined alongside the events of ordinary family life that were happening at the same time. 'At the very time you were betraying me with this person, this is what you were saying and doing ...' The more extended the affair, the more unravelling and reconstruction of the past has to be undertaken. Sometimes the process is so overwhelming that consciousness blocks it out temporarily. The clicking into place may occur only during sleep, jolting the person into a sudden, heart-thumping wakefulness in the middle of the night.

There is a growing panic about the future of the relationship. Does the partner intend to leave you? Given the force of your feelings, will you have no choice but to leave the relationship yourself? The trouble is that it is almost impossible to predict what effects an affair will have on any of the people involved. Affairs constitute a potentially serious threat to primary attachments. And interfering with primary attachments is playing with fire.

It is in the nature of the attachment system in children and adults that when attachment is fully established, it becomes quiescent, receding into the psychological background. Securely attached children seem to play as if they were not aware of whether their parent is there or not. Yet, if the parent moves beyond a certain zone of 'felt security', the child becomes alarmed. Similarly, adult relationships that seem to have settled into near indifference can spark into unexpected turmoil when the threat of abandonment by either partner reveals hidden dependencies.

From infancy on, we all select a primary attachment figure, a special number-one person. This is the person to whom we want to be close; from whom we object to being separated; to whom we return, as a 'safe haven', when we are distressed or in need of comfort, and who acts as a 'secure base' for us, giving us the confidence to go out and manage the world. In childhood, the primary attachment figure is normally the mother. In adulthood, it is the sexual partner in a long-term relationship.

An affair breaks that exclusive sexual bond and threatens to undo all the other elements of the relationship as well — the big and little intimacies that signal that the partner cares about you and is available to you. Like an abandoned child, the adult can experience a profound panic, a feeling of desolation and an overwhelming desire to be physically reunited with that special person, the only person in the world who can provide that feeling of safety, that everything is all right again.

When a child who has been temporarily separated from his parents is reunited with them, he is angry at them for having left, happy that they have returned, and fearful that they will leave again — a complex set of emotions that is difficult to manage. Similarly, the injured party in an adult relationship is torn by conflicting feelings — desperately needing reassurance in physical and sexual contact with the unfaithful partner, while at the same time feeling mounting rage at the partner and self-hate for having such needs at all.

The injured party has to confront multiple losses: loss of face or status with those who know about the affair (and all the agonising about how many people know, and when they knew); loss of control and predictability; loss of time and attention from the partner; loss of territory to the third party. The third party now assumes a psychological reality within the relationship and provokes one of the most powerful and primitive emotions — jealousy. Sexual jealousy is particularly corrosive to self-esteem.

In the middle of this maelstrom of feelings, decisions must be taken about how to handle the discovery of the affair. The reaction has to be decisive. Having discovered the affair, you must mark the spot, as it were, by withdrawing cooperation from the relationship, at least for a while. Depending on the seriousness of the affair and the domestic circumstances, this withdrawal can mean either partner leaving the home, at least temporarily. The effect of this withdrawal is that the guilty partner will now experience loss. Until there is some mutuality of loss, the injured party will not be able to negotiate a re-entry into the relationship on new terms. The immediate ending of the affair must be a first condition.

While trying to understand the erring partner's motivation may be important in the medium term, it is not helpful at this stage. Neither is it a good idea to be heroic or saintly. Studies show that cooperative behaviour on the part of the injured partner can increase, rather than decrease, exploitation by the other person. In fact, argument, protest, disagreement and a full show of intense feelings may be important steps in resolving the conflict and in re-establishing intimacy. No real dialogue is possible until the partner who had the affair begins to understand the other's experience of betrayal, and together they find ways to deal with that.

Jealousy generates an intense feeling of having been excluded. There is a great need to talk, to understand, to find out all the details. This is a very delicate issue. It is important for the wronged partner to find out some 'secrets' regarding the intimacies of the affair. This is part of the psychological process of re-establishing the original exclusive bond between the couple, of violating the exclusiveness of the affair, of excluding the third party. But too many details can be counter-productive and are often just a way for the unfaithful partner to offload his or her guilt.

The couple are then faced with the painstaking task of

rebuilding trust in each other and in the relationship. If they succeed in healing the wound of betrayal, they can achieve an altogether deeper and more mature intimacy than was ever possible before.

Dangerous Liaisons

Affairs are always newsworthy. At least once a year the airways resound with stories of affairs. Heartbroken wives, distraught husbands, despairing 'other women' all seeking to understand the mayhem in their lives. The lovers often feel that they are in the grip of a dream or a nightmare, depending on the stage of the affair. They often wake up in the night wondering how they brought all this on themselves. Where did it all begin? The parties frequently refer to the affair 'happening', but from my own observations, far from being mad impulses, affairs are choreographed as elaborately as a ballet.

The lead up

There is always a particular point when the germ of the idea for the affair is planted. This often consists of a step into somebody's private space — an intimate glance, an unexpected touch, a personal disclosure (how he really feels about you as a person, how she really feels about an important relationship). This is the opening move. The object of this attempt at a new closeness may be flattered. Both parties experience a frisson of excitement. After the encounter, each will look in the mirror with new interest and a certain smugness. 'Well now, who'd have thought …'

Spending more time together

The parties contrive to spend more time together. This is often disguised as high virtue: helping out a colleague at work who is 'having a lot of personal problems' (the favourite explanation for spending a lot of time with somebody who is junior in status) or 'is under awful pressure' (in the case of a senior person).

One or both parties begin to pay great attention to personal appearance — on the off-chance that they will meet each other. Spouses may notice the change but will be fobbed off with explanations about 'the need to get back into shape', health concerns and so on. The parties find themselves fantasising a lot about each other. In fantasy, it is the other person who makes the first sexual move. This reduces guilt feelings. The fantasising may lead to a generally heightened arousal and a new interest in sex. Initially, the unsuspecting spouse may be the beneficiary of this sexual enthusiasm, attributing it to the recently embarked-on programmes of fitness and grooming.

So far, so innocent. A lot of harmless flirting ends here when the parties get bored, get sense or get scared. The potential affair is aborted.

The beginning

The more determined continue the assiduous preparations. More and more opportunities to spend time together are created. This phase is characterised by one of two strategies. Each party drops all mention of the other's name to colleagues and, more particularly, at home. Queries by the spouse as to where so-and-so is — 'You haven't mentioned him/her for ages' — are greeted by a perplexed 'Who?', pretended indifference, or an offhand, slightly negative remark. Alternatively, there may be a gradual but persistent attempt to bring the other party's name into regular, boring conversations. This is an attempt to normalise the budding relationship, to make it sound like dull routine life. 'Nothing new going on here' is the message.

Getting to know me

The increased time together is accompanied by more self-disclosure. The true story of your unhappy marriage is the most tried and trusted procedure here. A more subtle and fashionable routine involves a ringing declaration of commitment to your marriage: 'We have a very strong and unusual relationship. My wife/husband is a wonderful person. We allow each other a lot of space.' There is also a lot of mutual flattery. 'I have never met anybody like you in my life … You have such dynamism/understanding/sensitivity/insight'. The flattery, to work, has to address what the target believes to be his/her own true nature. If this happens to be some quality that is ignored or unappreciated by the spouse, the flattery is experienced as a profound and long-awaited acknowledgment of the real 'you'.

One or both parties may refer obliquely to a past romantic disappointment or to a present lack in their lives. But the details will be severely censored until a later phase. Creating a favourable impression ('I can handle myself') is still the major goal. The parties' deepest feelings about the nature of true love, commitment and desire get a good airing. Conversations are full of exclamations like 'That is exactly how I feel! … You know what? It's amazing. You seem to think exactly like I do!'

Picking the moment

All that remains now is to pick the moment to make a sexual advance. This is less significant than it sounds. It is often accidental, frequently clumsy, but nearly always very exciting. The fact that it is illicit, that the pair have been leading up to it and fantasising about it for maybe months adds to the rush of adrenalin. This is frequently mistaken for complete sexual mutuality or even sexual destiny.

Settling in

The affair proper has two stages. The first is romantic, often involving planning adventures together. Weekends away are popular, often involving alarming risk-taking and vast expenditure. The parties go into (often enjoyable) hysterics about the near misses. Sex is good-to-wonderful, often occurring in odd locations, not so much due to unbridled desire as to a kind of daredevil playing hookey, a childish glee ('We can do what we like when they are not looking'). All this risk-taking may be relayed to an awed audience of best friends, further adding to the excitement.

Meanwhile, back home, the spouse may notice a change in the erring partner's demeanour. To cover his/her tracks, there may be an uncharacteristic cooperativeness, none of the usual rows about taking out the bins or spending money. The spouse may be urged to take up a hobby, get out more. Alternatively, there may be an uncharacteristic irritability, lots of seemingly irrational rows with the guilty party storming out in high dudgeon, thereby assuaging his/her conscience on the way to meet the lover.

The second stage is more serious and less fun. Getting away regularly becomes difficult and begins to involve an awful lot of lying. Elaborate cover-ups are necessary. Money becomes tight. The parties start wondering if it is worth all the risk-taking and effort. But the lovers have already begun to establish little routines and intimacies. It becomes hard to think of life without the other, although at this stage no plans for the future are entertained or even mentioned. The theme is still 'We are both adults and know what we are doing. Right?'

The crisis

The inevitable crisis arises from the increased involvement of each party in the affair. One or both of the parties is beginning to feel under pressure from the psychological conflicts engendered by the affair. These include anxiety about living a double life, guilt about the spouse or children or a growing fear that the other party is getting too involved or demanding. Alternatively, the conflicts may stem from one party's growing involvement and corresponding uncertainty about the commitment of the other. This uncertainty breeds a fierce desire for action and decisions.

This crisis of commitment can be provoked by almost anything. A pregnancy (real or imagined) or Being Found Out are the most dramatic. Often the crisis has been subconsciously manipulated. The parties have become preoccupied, careless. The first big row occurs. If the pair cannot resolve the underlying issues, they cannot go on to the final phase: ending either the affair or the marriage(s). If the decision is to leave the marriage, the next task is telling the spouse. This very often takes an unforseeably long time to implement and makes the lover very edgy. The married party will frequently baulk at the last minute and will come back to the lover with increasingly lame excuses.

Different strategies are employed for the moment of truth. The weak-willed or the very guilty may never face the spouse. Instead, they leave and send a letter; or worse, get the lover to tell the spouse. The braver souls tell and wait. The resulting emotional blow-out sometimes makes the offending spouse so panicky, guilty, moved or impressed by the spouse's depth of feeling that a reconciliation becomes possible. In this case, he/she now has to go back and tell the lover of the change of plan. Repeat Scene with lover.

Moral. Stop at Stage One. Stick to the fantasies.

Trust

Trust has been defined as the confidence that you will find in someone else what you desire, rather than what you fear. From the very beginning of life, it is the most basic psychological issue to be resolved. If the needs of a child are responded to consistently, predictably and with love, then the parent, and later the world itself, are perceived to be benevolent and trustworthy. And, just as important, the child comes to believe that he or she is the kind of person the world responds to in a helpful way. Thus, the growth of trust and self-esteem proceed in tandem.

Of course, there is inevitable disappointment and conflict in early relationships, because no parent is perfect. As long as the child is not frequently left needy and distressed, then the frustrations will not be overwhelming and can be accommodated by the developing self.

If, on the other hand, the frustrations are constant, then the child comes to be dominated by its own needs. Feelings of rage and anxiety overwhelm the still fragile self. If needs are met only unpredictably, the child can form no consistent image of the parent, and by extension, the world. Will it be a good day or a bad day? Will I be comforted or ignored? Can I depend on others when it really counts? The image of the parent remains fragmented: full of frustration one day, relief and ease the next. Instead of a core of trust developing, there is a yawning vacuum of disappointment.

These early relationships seem to act as templates for later adult relationships. Trust is the first bridge we build to other people and the world. If that bridge is not sound, then every step closer to another in an intimate relationship is fraught with danger.

Trust is not gullibility. Gullible people tend to be so insecure and lonely, to need somebody to lean on so badly, that they place inappropriate confidence in others, sometimes in the face of contrary evidence. For example, a strong desire for excessive intimacy may reflect a lack of trust just as much as an extreme desire for self-sufficiency. People who are capable of a high level of trust are not gullible. They make an act of trust because they feel it is the right thing to do in the circumstances, even though they are aware of the risks. In effect, high-trust people maintain confidence in others until there is clear evidence to the contrary, whereas low-trust people cannot place any confidence in others until there is cast-iron evidence.

The critical role that trust plays in the workings of relationships was shown in recent studies of how different couples react to positive and negative events in their relationships. The couples were categorised into those who had a high degree of trust in each other, those who felt uncertain, and those who actively mistrusted each other.

Predictably, those couples who actively mistrusted each other reacted badly to situations where they were let down by their partners. Each disappointment seemed to trigger negative memories, painfully reminding them of other examples of the risks involved in depending on the partner's good intentions. Even positive behaviour on the part of the partner was viewed with suspicion and thus had little impact on the relationship. To protect themselves from disappointment, they had already retreated from depending on each other, thus further removing the opportunity to rebuild trust by showing care and concern.

Couples who were uncertain about each other reacted favourably when their partners responded well to them in the context of some crisis or problem. Yet they were unable to feel more confident about their partner's motives, setting ever higher standards of proof of the other's good intentions (e.g. 'Yes, that was very nice of him, but of course it does not prove he really cares about me. To prove that, he would have to behave like that every day.') It is as if the prospect of a partner being responsive almost frightens them and certainly does not reassure them. They pull back, afraid their hopes will not be met, feeling something approaching despair about the prospect of fulfilment.

When their partners actually let them down, the uncertain couples reacted very negatively, and construed partners' motives in a very dark way.

This readiness to rush to judgment on the partner was in stark contrast to their reluctance to grant any credit for the partner's positive behaviour. They seemed to store positive and negative experiences of the partner into different compartments, just as the child who is cared for unpredictably cannot form a unified image of the good or bad parent. As a consequence, the uncertain couples had great difficulty putting a negative experience into perspective. It is as if they are primed to perceive threats more easily than promise. They are thus trapped in their conflicts and ambivalence, constructing a way of dealing with the world that feeds their fears and undermines their hopes. They are not so much constantly testing to see if the partner cares, as testing if the partner is again going to let them down.

The third group of couples, those who trusted each other, reacted positively when their partners responded to them in a caring way in a crisis. Unexpectedly, they responded most positively of all to negative events, expressing even more confidence about their partner's good intentions even when their partner had let them down in a particular situation. They did not allow their disappointment to undermine their trust in the partner. Instead, they seemed to defend against the threat posed by bad behaviour by actively reaching back into their store of good feelings, which resulted in a further consolidation of their positive attitudes about the relationship. In fact, the partner's failings served to remind them of the partner's virtues.

High-trust couples seem to have developed a relatively unified core of feelings about their partners. Hopes and fears are not separated or split into positive and negative compartments. The partner's basic motivation is not easily open to question. Lapses in behaviour are discounted in advance and are thus more readily endured (e.g. 'I know that he really cares about me, so what else could be the reason he let me down on this occasion?').

Trust seems to have a critical role to play in constructing an overall positive mental structure which can then absorb negative experiences. Trust appears to operate like a good 'internal mother', warding off threats, cushioning the impact of negative events, and hastening recovery from distress. By not constantly questioning their partner's basic motivation, by relegating the inevitable disappointments in a relationship to a less important domain and not allowing them threaten the central core of attachment and love, high-trust couples create an intimate life that is free from continual uncertainty. These are lessons that even the most distressed couples could learn.

The Unhappy Couple, On the Other Hand ...

In the United States, where they measure such things, it has been found that couples who describe themselves as satisfied spend about sixteen hours a year in conflict, whereas dissatisfied couples spent about 180 hours a year arguing with each other. Heated conflicts were both more frequent (three per month versus 1.3 per month) and lasted longer (just over five hours versus a half an hour) for dissatisfied, as opposed to satisfied, couples.

Psychologists who study couples believe that even two relatively neurotic individuals can and do have happy marriages. What very often distinguishes unhappy couples from their happier counterparts are negative, self-perpetuating interaction patterns. Among unhappy couples there are more intense negative feelings expressed: more anger, contempt, insults, fear, disgust, criticism, complaining. There is also more reciprocity of negative feelings. As soon as one partner starts, the other quickly responds in kind.

Both happy and unhappy couples row about the same things: money, raising children, the allocation of household chores. But while happy couples row about these issues only sometimes, unhappy couples row about them all the time. In addition, unhappy couples frequently squabble about communication, sex and each other's personality characteristics. Thus they argue about how little they talk to each other and about the way they talk to each other. They accuse each other of not listening and of interrupting.

They argue about the frequency of sex, the way they have sex, and about whether the woman is taking enough sexual initiative.

They complain about each other's personality characteristics: one frequently accusing the other of trying to dominate them, neglecting them and not sticking to agreements. Women complain that they do not have enough 'space' for their own interests and personal development.

The fact that they row so often about the same topics shows that they are chronically unable to reach a resolution. They get stuck. Psychologists have identified just how this happens.

When any couple are discussing an issue between them, there are three distinct phases: agenda-building, arguing and negotiation. The first phase is for setting up the agenda, the goal being to get the issues on the table, as they are viewed by each of the partners. The second phase is the arguing phase. The goal is for each partner to argue energetically for their points of view and to understand the points of disagreement between them. The third phase is the negotiation phase, and its goal is compromise.

It is possible to find differences between happy and unhappy couples in the way they interact during each of these phases. For example, in the agenda-building phase, unhappy couples use what psychologists call 'cross-complaining' patterns:

Woman: I've had an exhausting day with the children. I haven't stopped working since you left this morning.
Man: You think you're tired. I'm ready to drop. I just want to flop in front of the TV.

Happy couples, on the other hand, use what is called a 'validating' pattern:

Woman: I've had an exhausting day with the children.
Man: Oh, you poor thing. Bad was it?
Woman: Yeah. How was your day?
Man: Exhausting. I just want to flop in front of the TV.
Woman: Uh mmm. I know.

In the cross-complaining pattern, neither partner can get their concerns (i.e. how tired they feel) properly accepted on the agenda. What each wants is some acknowledgment of their complaint and an expression of sympathy. Thus buoyed, there is some hope each can respond to the other. This is what the other couple achieve by 'validating' each other's point of view.

In the negotiation phase, there are also clear differences. Unhappy couples immediately follow a proposal from one partner by a counter-proposal from the other.

Man: I did the school run all last week. This week I think you should do it.
Woman: Well, I can't do it Thursday. I'll do it next week instead. You do it again this week, will you?
Man: No. I did it last week.
Woman: I told you. I can't do it Thursday. You're expecting me to do something I can't do.

Happy couples react differently. They follow a proposal from one partner by some acknowledgment of its validity and maybe a suggested compromise.

Man: I did the school runs all last week.
Woman: Uh mmm, I know.
Man: Will you do it this week?
Woman: OK, fair enough. I'm not sure about Thursday, but we can work something out.

In the middle phase, the arguing phase, happy and unhappy couples are indistinguishable except for their non-verbal behaviour. Happy couples continually intersperse non-verbal forms of agreement into their communication: smiling and murmuring (yeah, right, Uh mmm, I know). These are clear signals to the partner that you are listening, 'tracking'. They do not necessarily communicate agreement with the partner's point of view, but they communicate that you are on their side, prepared to accept that it might make sense to see things the way they do.

The unhappy couples meanwhile are accompanying their interactions with negative, or at best neutral, non-verbal behaviour: sighing, and sighing 'with the whole body' (slumping), fumbling, tense posture and facial expression, inattention, gaze avoidance, as well as pointing, jabbing and slicing hand gestures. Distressed couples are adept at reading these non-verbal signals, prompting accusations like 'You are not listening ... you're getting irritated now ... you're on the defensive as usual ... I can see already you are preparing your reply ... you're closing yourself off.'

All this intensifies the air of conflict and the negative feelings. Most revealing of all is the finding that unhappy couples, once they begin to comment on each other's non-verbal behaviour in the middle of an argument, become preoccupied by it. They forget the original issue between them and fail to achieve any resolution. In contrast, happy couples will comment on each other's non-verbal behaviour briefly, but will not be deflected from resolving the issue at hand.

Man: I can tell you're not listening to me. You were miles away.

Woman: Was I? Sorry. What were you saying?

The unhappy couples, on the other hand, get caught up in an endless cycle of criticism, denial and extension of the argument.

Woman: I can tell you're not listening.

Man: Well, if you stopped talking for a change, I might be more inclined to listen occasionally.

Woman: Oh, that's rich coming from the man who loves the sound of his own voice.

Man: Just as well, otherwise you'd walk all over me.

Woman: Well, if you think that talking me down will get me to listen, you're all wrong.

Man: You don't listen anyway.

And so on. There seems to be no obvious exit from the argument.

Whatever the origin of such patterns, or the individual motivation behind them, the first step to putting them right is to be aware of them, to recognise that these destructive patterns are joint problems. Even if only one partner changes their contribution, the pattern cannot continue. In the most distressed relationship, to change the deadly choreography of one such pattern will have a powerful impact.

When Love Breaks Down

Very often when a well-established partnership breaks down, triggered by what may seem like a minor event, there is a sense of shock. One, perhaps both, of the partners, and almost all observers, are caught by surprise. 'What happened?' people ask, 'They seemed to get on so well — the perfect couple?' The mystery is how the commitment to the partnership could be eroded without at least one party having been aware of what was happening. One bewildered partner will say, 'I had no idea that things had changed until one day she told me she was leaving.' The other will say with equal bewilderment 'I woke one day and I suddenly realised that it was all over. I don't know why I did not realise it before. This relationship was finished a long time ago.' What are the signposts on the road to dissolution? Dismantling a major commitment is not a single event. Rather, it is an extended process with distinct psychological stages. Indeed, progress through these stages can be observed in the dissolution of just about any kind of partnership — personal, business or political.

Stage One: The first stage involves the gradual, often imperceptible, erosion of the original basis for commitment to the partnership. One partner carries out a series of small actions that are increasingly at variance with the nature of the commitment, the 'understanding' between the couple. The significance of these actions is gradually borne in on the other partner. The acts can be sins of commission or omission: taking unilateral action on something that normally would have been a joint decision; a disrespectful attitude or comment; forgetting an important ritual in the relationship. The defining characteristic of these incidents is that, despite their overt insignificance, they create a feeling of betrayal, a breach of trust.

Such actions become more frequent, but in small, inconspicuous increments. Of course, isolated breaches of trust or mutual understanding also happen in well-functioning relationships, but with the crucial difference that the strong feelings which they provoke are taken seriously and serve as the first line of defence both against a repetition and against the further development of the breakdown. Feelings of guilt and shame on the part of the erring partner, and jealousy, anger and anguish on the part of the injured partner, will be used to flag the danger. Contrition and promises to do better in the future reinstate the understanding. Of course, in some partnerships there is more than one erring party.

These first defences will fail if one partner's self-interest has grown so big that it shuts out or obscures the reality of the other partner's feelings or character. In that case, small acts of betrayal, and the unresolved conflicts they generate, will continue. For the moment, however, there will be no dramatic, emotional consequences; overall attachments and the commitment remain stable. But there is a new vigilance about the partner and the equity in the relationship.

Stage Two: Partners are still generally unprepared for the fact that the basis for a further gradual erosion of trust has now been laid. If the process continues, a new stage will be reached where their feelings suddenly change. That transition is like a stone rolling down a gentle slope for a while and then suddenly picking up speed as it goes over a cliff. This stage is heralded by the realisation that the situation is becoming intolerable. The partner enters a period of emotional ambivalence, a revival of old suspicions and doubts about the other. Such doubts and suspicions are usually the same ones that arose at a much earlier stage of the relationship, just before a major commitment was made (e.g. pre-wedding/signing-on-for-the-partnership nerves). But this is still a very private anguish. The result is not an immediate confrontation with the partner, but the beginning of a kind of brooding disengagement, characterised by self-doubts, recrimination, indecision and negativity in how self, partner and life in general are viewed. If this brooding continues, it may lead to a crisis, even if there are no further 'objective' major acts of betrayal.

Communication patterns may change subtly, reflecting the greater distance between the partners (e.g. more gaze avoidance, more use of 'I' and less of 'we'). There may be 'leaking' of negative feelings into interactions with the partner: sudden, apparently irrational bouts of irritability or argumentativeness — which may provide the erring partner with an excuse to rationalise his or her behaviour and to abandon attempts at repairing the relationship ('He's impossible to please anyway. There's no point trying to improve things.')

Stage Three: The next stage is ushered in by the feeling 'I must do something about this'. The stress, agitation and ambivalence become so great that there is increasing internal pressure to confront the partner. Anxieties centre on how to put one's own case and how the partner is likely to react — whether the confrontation will help to repair the relationship or will make matters worse. The goal is to get satisfactory explanations from the partner and to redefine and repair the relationship. The focus now is on the 'relationship' ('what has gone wrong with our relationship'), rather than the partner ('why is he treating me this way?').

Since by now one partner is distinctly aggrieved and hostile, and the other is probably feeling threatened or guilty, communication tends to be tense. The erring partner may resolve to put things right and, if this happens to the other's satisfaction, the process of breakdown stops here. Or the erring partner may be unwilling or unable to put things right, often denying that there is a problem. The aggrieved partner's determination to push for a resolution of the problems may be undermined by the realisation that the attachment to the partner is still strong and by a growing fear that they may lose the relationship.

This may then usher in a period of oscillation between intense reconciliations and angry withdrawal, between hope and despair. The partners find themselves swinging between emotional extremes. A major crisis is impending, even though it is developing slowly. The couple are tumbling down the slope, but occasionally succeed in scrambling back a few inches. If they can struggle back to the previous confrontation stage, the crisis may be resolved. If they do not succeed, one or both partners may begin to form the view that the negative aspects are outweighing the positive aspects of the relationship and begin to seriously consider if they would be better off without it.

There may be increased fantasy about alternatives to the relationship. The possibility of repairing the relationship may be gradually abandoned and what was once merely ambivalence is now replaced by a sustained, coherent, negative account of the relationship. Each partner begins privately to rehearse a 'public story' about the cause of the breakdown. Finding a way to escape blame becomes a major preoccupation. What were once seen as minor flaws in the relationship, for example, are now described as fatal weaknesses that were destined to bring down the relationship.

Stage Four: All the rumination and talk of withdrawal now culminates in a determination to end the partnership. The new concern is how best to manage the personal, social and public consequences of the dissolution. Possible losses of status, network support and security for the future must be dealt with. The personal dynamics between the partners now are superseded by the social network as the significant base and background to the dissolving relationship. How to tell friends, supporters and the general public about the break-up becomes a pressing concern. The 'public story' already prepared and rehearsed in private by each partner must be moulded to fit in with prevailing cultural values. Gossip and taking sides become crucial components in the process of assigning blame and saving face.

While the public face may look resolved and strong, the private feelings are usually predominantly of loss, and the psychological work is mourning. Worries about one's own personal future surface frequently. The prevailingly negative account often falters as it fights to overcome what was once a strong commitment. Unruly feelings of attachment reassert themselves and this new ambivalence centres on the memories of past achievements and happier times. But the feelings of loss are further deepened by the realisation that the break-up is now inevitable.

Stage Five: The novelist John Fowles, describing the ending of a relationship, wrote: 'Such changes ... don't announce themselves dramatically; they steal slowly over months, masking themselves behind reconciliations, periods of happiness, new resolves. Like some form of lethal disease, they invite every myth of comforting explanation before they exact the truth.'

The fifth stage of dissolution is the slow process of exacting that truth. In the aftermath of a major commitment, though people may feel that they have done the right thing in ending that commitment, they find themselves engaged in an obsessive review of past events. The ultimate goal may now be to recover from the loss of a vital commitment and to begin the process of seeking new ones. But first a fuller personal story of the relationship must be constructed which goes beyond simply assigning blame and saving face. The story must have a beginning, a middle and an end. The good memories as well as the bad ones must be integrated into the account of what really happened. Only then can it be consigned to the past.

Most important, the moral of the tale must be found. Otherwise it will simply be too demoralising to turn to the future and start again.

Changing Social Trends in Family Life

This week three middle-aged parents, who had never dreamt that they would be touched by such social change, told me that their daughters had become single mothers. 'But', each added quickly 'she is in a long-term, stable relationship'.

These mildly shell-shocked parents did not even mention marriage, adopting instead the rhetoric of the young. It was yet another indication that there is a revolution underway in personal relationships and that it is here to stay.

It is something to mull over in this [1994], the Year of the Family, because the year got off to a bad start. First we had the British cabinet member with his two love children. If he left his wife and went to live with his lover and their child, which family, the old one or the new one, did we all want to strengthen?

Then we had the possibility of babies with up to five parents: a sperm donor, an egg donor, the woman providing the womb for pregnancy, and the couple who will rear the child — let alone any additional step-parents acquired through separation and second relationships. Or the intergenerational complications: we heard about the egg of a granny, fertilised by an ex-husband and given to a divorced daughter.

So what do we mean by 'the family' these days? The benchmark family, against which all other groupings are measured, involves a relationship between a husband and a wife that is legal, permanent, sexually exclusive, and reproductive. Add to that the lingering ideal of a full-time mother and homemaker and a lifelong 'good provider' father and what you have is a powerful archetype. Yet almost every defining characteristic in this standard package has been challenged or changed in the past decade.

Take the traditional bargain between women and men of an

exchange of sex for marriage. There is now sex before, outside and after marriage. This revolution is carrying in its wake profound social changes with regard to cohabitation, birth outside marriage, marital breakdown, and second or 'blended' families. Do these social changes, along with breakthroughs in reproductive medicine, mean that it is no longer possible to identify what constitutes a family?

Experts on the family disagree on the prospects for the future. The pessimists see these changes as symptoms of a terminal disintegration. The family, they believe, has been seriously weakened by the social experimentation made possible by the sexual revolution, and by an increasing cultural acceptance that when parenting competes with other adult interests and roles, self-interest is legitimate and self-sacrifice is out.

In today's world, a generation of children is growing up with no fathers. Evidence from studies in the United States shows that more than half of all those children whose parents separated had had no contact whatsoever with their fathers for a year. More than one-third had had no contact for at least five years. There is growing unease, too, about the long-term welfare of babies born to teenage mothers — single, struggling with the pressure of low income, incomplete formal education and no male partner to share the responsibilities of parenting. There are even veiled arguments that, while single parenthood and second relationships may be manageable, choices of particular lifestyles for middle-class, well-educated people, they translate into social chaos among the poor.

But other family scholars are taking a more optimistic view. They point out that the archetypal family has never represented reality as closely as we think. There were always out-of-wedlock births, albeit on a smaller scale than today. Only the socially prescribed solutions were different, more hidden: adoption, institutionalisation and forced marriage. Marriages have always broken down, men have always strayed, children have always been abused and neglected. It is just that these failures are now out in the open. We have redefined private dilemmas as social problems, swapped internal agony for social tumult.

Feminists point out that 'the family' was always shorthand for nurturing, and nurturing was always shorthand for mothering. And women are still doing most of that, whether on their own or with a man. In that sense, family values — women nurturing — have not changed all that much. The difference is that women can set the agenda more, can decide the precise circumstances in which they will love and mother. In other words, the struggle for equality is at the core of current family turmoil. But this is productive conflict and family life will ultimately be the better for it.

The more optimistic family scholars believe that changes in the archetypal family structure are not synonymous with social and psychological disintegration. The politics of stability, where success is construed as getting married and staying married at all costs, are increasingly out of synch with how real people make choices about love and happiness. Young people no longer believe that the tidy conventional solution of love, marriage and baby carriage is always best for them. The starting point today is to secure a close and intimate relationship, with communication the key to its functioning. The other ingredients of the traditional family are added on, or not, as the young people themselves mature and their relationship develops. Thus, over time, they may add economic partnership, parenthood, legal status. But the order in which they do these things is increasingly under individual, rather than social, control. Appearances, legal status, respectability have moved down the list of priorities.

I would like to believe the more optimistic vision of future family life.

Women and Men

Don't You Know that It's Different for Girls?

Anyone who has tried to get the girls to play with the boys, or the boys with the girls, will have discovered the remarkable resistance of both sexes to such a politically correct parental plan. Occasionally, if there is absolutely no other same-sex friend around, boys and girls will agree to play together. But, in nearly all cultures, girls prefer to play with girls, and boys with boys. Why?

The explanation seems to be that boys and girls primarily look to their own peer groups as they try to learn their gender roles. Girls not only practise being girls with each other, but seem almost to define themselves in opposition to boys. This is true of boys to an even greater extent: they are more preoccupied than girls with the need to remain separate and different from the opposite sex. In other words, you learn to be a boy by not doing what girls do. And vice versa.

From early childhood, a boy seems to approach the world as an individual who is conscious of a hierarchical order in which he is one-up or one-down. Life is seen as a contest in which he has to struggle to keep his status and preserve his independence. A girl, on the other hand, approaches the world as an individual in a network of attachments. She has to struggle to maintain closeness and to avoid isolation. Children's play reflects these different agendas.

Boys play in large groups and their play is rougher and takes up more space. They play more in public spaces. Their friendships are organised around shared interests in activities. They are very concerned about who is dominant. They constantly interrupt each other, boast, issue orders or refuse to comply with each other. They repeatedly stop games to argue about rules. They compete to hold the floor, telling jokes and stories, heckling each other and generally taking each other down a peg or two with great glee. Boys measure their status by carefully tracking who is giving orders and who is taking them. They jealously guard their independence, that is, their freedom from being told what to do. Boys' style of interaction has been described as restrictive: it tends to derail whatever interaction is going on, inhibiting or causing the partner to withdraw. It is male concern with dominance — that is, not showing weakness in front of other men and boys — that is believed to underlie this restrictive style.

With all this competition, how do boys function well together? Boys seem to develop group structures — the well-defined roles and rules of hierarchies — to set limits on male aggression. The struggle for dominance is regulated by the group structure. The chief commodity that is bartered in male hierarchies is status. The rules for achieving it are clear. In other words, boys and men probably need group structures more than girls and women do in order to preserve cohesion.

Girls organise themselves differently. They tend to form close, intimate friendships with one or two other girls, and to congregate in each others' homes or gardens. They share confidences with each other and become very emotional when friendships break up. They tend to express agreement with what another girl has just said, pause to give each other a chance to speak, and acknowledge points made by others. Conversation for them is not a competition, but a socially binding process. They try to tone down conflicts. This is not to say that girls do not try to get their own way. Far from it. But they try to get their own way in a manner quite different from boys.

Girls have a double agenda: (1) they want to be liked; (2) they want to get their own way. Boys simply want to get their own way. Boys try to prevail by appealing to rules and using threats. Girls rarely challenge each other. They make suggestions, use evasion and negotiate compromises. For example, rather than ordering another child to give up the swing, a girl will tell her that a third child, not herself, wants it. When conflicts break out about how a game is being played, girls will not bother arguing for very long about the rules. They will change the game. Their primary aim is to restore harmonious group functioning, not to right a wrong or to establish a principle. Intimacy, not status, is what is being constantly monitored. Girls are not on the look-out for overt one-upmanship, but for subtle shifts in alliance. They measure their relationships in terms of how close, or not close, they are to other girls. Boasting or explicit attempts at dominance are punished as 'showing off' or 'being bossy' and decrease closeness. Intimacy is to do with being close and being the same — these are the things which keeps the interaction or the relationships going.

In adult life, men naturally tend to import into mixed-sex groups the same techniques that were successful in all-male groups. They do more initiating, directing, interrupting. They talk louder and tend to lose interest when women talk. As a con-sequence of all this assertiveness, they wield more influence in groups. In addition, since the worlds of work, sport and politics are generally organised in hierarchies by and for men, women have the choice of either adopting men's style, which is foreign to them, or of carrying on the way they do with other women: smiling, agreeing, being attentive, providing what has been called 'silent applause' — with predictable results.

Does that mean that women cannot function in groups? No. All-women groups, for example, have more success than all-male groups in tasks that require discussion and negotiating, whereas all-male groups do better with tasks where success depends on the volume of ideas generated. But when both women and men debate in a group, the men's self-esteem rises and, afterwards, they like their women opponents better. For women, the reverse is true. Their self-esteem falls and they like the men less.

Men show the greatest resistance to influence in group situ-ations when they feel they are under surveillance by other men. They do not want other men to know that they have yielded to another person, especially a woman, in case it might be inter-preted as a weakness. In one-to-one situations with women, men tend to be more accommodating because they are freed from the one-upmanship which characterises groups containing men. If women had the power to organise how they go about their work, it seems they would be well advised to cultivate mutually productive one-to-one relationships when they have to work with men, to use all-women groups whenever possible, and only to enter mixed-sex groups after a stiff drink.

Vive la Différence?

In terms of intellectual and personality attributes, are men and women the same? Sometime in the early 1970s, researchers who had been studying differences between the sexes sent up the white smoke: we have an answer: yes, they are. True, a few differences were found. Men did a little better on tests of mathematics and spatial ability, and women came out better on tests of verbal ability. Men were found to be more often than women both agents and victims of aggression. Since that time, the picture has remained relatively unchanged.

By the early 1990s, the general conclusion that men and women are similar in terms of personality and social behaviour has been challenged by one of the leading researchers in the field. It turns out that individuals behave differently depending on whether they are with members of the same sex or the opposite sex. This emerged when researchers observed that children behaved very differently depending on whether they were with a same-sex friend or with an opposite-sex friend. For example, when observers counted the number of times a child simply stood passively watching another child play with toys, no major differences were found between boys and girls. However, when they are paired with a boy, the behaviour of girls is dramatically affected. Then, they frequently stand on the sidelines and let the boys monopolise the toys. Yet, when playing with other little girls, such passive behaviour seldom occurs. In fact, when girls play together, passive behaviour occurs less often than it does when boys play with each other. Moreover, when children as young as thirty-three months play with each other, boys and girls do much the same thing. They hug and push, grab and offer toys to one another, they invite each other to play, protest and issue orders. But when playing with a same-sex friend, they are much more socially active — that is, they do more of everything — than when they are with a child of the opposite sex. When asked to approach another child, children as young as three stop further away when the other child is of the opposite sex. They seem wary.

By pre-school stage, children spend nearly three times as much time with children of their own sex as with children of the opposite sex. By age six, they spend eleven times as much time. It might be thought that this segregation has to do with boys and girls liking to play different games. That is only part of the answer. Pre-school children, for example, spend a great deal of time engaged in activities that are gender-neutral. Even when attempts are made by adults to break down children's preferences for same-sex playmates, this pattern proves very resistant. In fact, it is now clear, even in co-educational schools, that when not under pressure from adults, children will spontaneously choose their own sex as friends.

How can this phenomenon of spontaneous sex segregation be explained? Many researchers believe that same-sex peer groups are the primary way that boys and girls learn their gender roles. Boys learn to be boys, to define themselves in comparison to other boys and in opposition to girls. The same is true of girls. But why such steadfast avoidance of each other?

Part of the reason seems to be that girls find it so difficult to influence boys. Even before the age of three, boys will not do what girls tell them to do, but are much more responsive to doing what another boy says. Girls use the same style of influence, that is, polite suggestion, which they have found works well for them with each other and with adults. Boys prefer and respond to what they have found is the only influence style that works with other boys — direct demands. And, as they grow up, boys become even more more resistant to polite suggestions. Clearly, girls get fed up interacting with people who will not respond to them, so they avoid boys.

Why do little boys refuse to be influenced by girls? Boys establish their status by telling other boys what to do. In games of 'Doctor', boys want to play the doctor role 79 per cent of the time and often get into long arguments with other boys about which boy will get this high-status role. Taking orders is a mark of low status. Naturally, boys resist being told what to do, especially by a girl. Girls, on the other hand, expect to influence and be influenced by others. They experience the world as a network of intimates. In games of doctor they ask each other what role they want. In the case of a dispute, they often make a joint proposal 'We'll both be doctors'.

It is not surprising that in the power politics of the boys' world, they have to invoke adult authority to survive. In one study, for example, children were observed competing for the use of a toy. When there was no adult present, the boys monopolised the toy. When an adult was present, the girls got at least equal access. This is why girls generally stick closer to adults than boys do. It used to be thought that this reflected girls' dependency. Not so, because it happens only when the boys are around. Girls simply found that boys were less aversive if there was an adult there to keep their dominance in check. In contrast, in all-girl groups, girls stood farther away from the adults than boys did in all-boy groups. In fact the girls, unlike the boys, actively maintained their distance from the adult, drawing further away when the adult moved towards them.

As children grow into adolescence and adulthood, this sexual apartheid begins to be dismantled, though young people continue to spend a great deal of time with same-sex friends. What happens when the products of such separate worlds interact with each other? Girls emerge from childhood with a well-developed style of interaction. They have been used to influencing each other by making suggestions, expressing agreements, generally helping to keep the interaction going — what has been described as an enabling style. Boys emerge from childhood well schooled in wielding influence by competing, threatening, giving direct orders, interrupting, all designed to get the partner to withdraw or submit. This style also tends to shorten or terminate interaction — what has been termed a restrictive style.

Suddenly, men find themselves with women partners who, unlike other males, are not constantly competing with them. While this might be a culture shock for boys, it is a pleasant one. Young women, meanwhile, are finding out once again that polite suggestion is not the way to exert influence on assertive, independent-minded young men. When they talk to each other, men and women have to learn to make adjustments, but women end up making more. This is why women are dissatisfied with communication in their relationships with men, while men, who are party to the same conversations, express themselves to be satisfied. This must be at least part of the reason that, in adolescence, women's self-esteem drops and depression rises. It is not until the relationship between a man and a woman becomes deep and enduring that issues of power and influence are resolved, although men continue to use more direct bargaining and women more indirect styles of influence.

Only a Pale Imitation of Mother

We all know that women are the superior sex when it comes to interest and skill in love, don't we? That women speak the language of love, intimacy and sharing of self with consummate fluency. That men are more preoccupied with doing and achieving rather than loving. That many men have no truly intimate relationships apart from the one with their wife or lover.

What then are we to make of the fact that studies consistently show that men fall in love faster than women and that they have more romantic attitudes to their partners than women do? For example, it is men rather than women who describe their relationship in terms such as 'we are perfect for each other' and who say that they would not marry someone they were not in love with, even if that person had all the other qualities they wanted. Men tend to see love as either magically and perfectly present, or totally absent.

Freud, an astute observer of men, if not always of women, believed that men love not wisely but too well. Only men are capable of that peculiarly intense state of being 'in love'. This is the sort of idealised love that has given rise, for example, to great love poetry and noble but doomed romances, which Freud described as 'suggestive of neurotic compulsion'. Women, in contrast, love in a more measured, realistic way. Their need lies not in a compulsion to love, but in a strong but clear-eyed desire to be loved.

In Freudian terms, the differences between men and women can be traced to the different psychological tasks faced by boys and girls in infancy. All of us start life in a state of primary narcissism. In other words, there are no firm boundaries between the self and the world. When needs for food, bodily closeness and comfort are met, there is an 'oceanic' feeling of being at one with the world. Only gradually does the infant become aware of a presence outside of the self — usually the mother, who is responsible for the child's feeding, care and protection. The original dynamic of psychological development is this early tension between narcissistic- or self-love and love for the mother. If the child is to develop a strong ego, it has to stay focussed on itself. Yet, in order to survive, it has to form a strong attachment to another person.

The child resolves that tension by transforming his original self-love — all the psychological energy originally invested in self — into love for another. The infant achieves this by by what Freud calls a process of 'over-valuation'. In other words, just as the child once fancied himself, in Freud's phrase, as 'His Majesty the Baby', the very centre and core of creation, the mother now becomes the idealised receptacle of this narcissistic energy. He projects his idealised self-image on to her.

I say 'he' advisedly since Freud believed this process reaches completion only in the case of males. Nonetheless, the leap from self-love to love of mother, the prototype of all later loves, is fraught with difficulties. For a boy, there is the additional leap of having to love a person who is fundamentally different from himself because the mother is the opposite sex. He has to project even more of himself on to her so that, by mirroring him, he can love her as himself.

The girl, on the other hand, can remain identified with her mother. Self-love and love of the mother can merge. Thus, Freud believed, women remain very interested in themselves in a narcissistic way. Very narcissistic women may hold a particular fascination for men, not only because such women are often beautiful, but because they represent for men the lost parts of self — that profound self-contentment and self-preoccupation of childhood which men have had to renounce. Freud believed that women can scale the dizzy heights of male, idealised love once they have a child, whom they can view as an extension of their bodies and themselves.

To understand the quality of love in men, it must be

remembered that they seek forever to regain that lost 'oceanic feeling', that bliss of complete sensual satisfaction that they experienced in infancy. That is why men are so ready to fall blindly in love, to exalt the beloved into a sexual ideal — some perfect combination of the powerful all-satisfying madonna of infancy, and the whore of illicit fantasies. Only in love, particularly in sexual love, can men regress and reclaim the lost parts of themselves. At the height of such love, the boundary between the I and the lover threatens to melt away. There is a feeling of limitlessness, of being at one with nature, a conviction that he and the lover are one; in other words, a regression to that infantile state before the 'I' was fully differentiated from the world. That process of regression, however, also leaves men open in their adult love relationships to the terrors of infancy — the possible intrusion of a more powerful male rival and the expulsion from Eden by the betrayal of a woman.

For a man to achieve even an approximation of his ideal love, he has to unite the two psychic currents — affection and sensuality. The affectionate current is the older one, the attachment to the care-giving mother. From the very beginning, it carries erotic overtones, but these have to be diverted and held over for adult sexual love. At puberty, the affectionate current is joined by the sensual current. With the driving force of both currents behind him, the adult man is capable of true adult intimacy. Sexual pleasure can incorporate the earlier childhood sensual experiences of the body's erogenous zones.

But when the mother exercises great attraction and power throughout the boy's childhood and adolescence, the fusion of the sensual and the affectionate currents when he becomes a man remains fraught with danger. Thus, some men can allow the sensual current to be aroused only by those women who do not resemble the forbidden parent. If a woman resembles that parent, she can evoke only affection, not arousal.

But, Freud gloomily concluded, even for the most integrated of men, the constant search, through sexuality, for the lost completeness and satiation of infancy is ultimately doomed. The lover, no matter how idealised, is only a surrogate for the original love. The endless search to replace it with substitutes will bring no complete satisfaction. Is that why men fall in and out of love so often, for many men why sexual intercourse is the most meaningful way of giving and receiving love? Are men always trying to regain a foothold in paradise lost?

Sometimes It's Hard To Be a Woman

Whenever women meet with a political agenda (national, local, social or gender-related), one issue, which seems to be unique to women-only gatherings, frequently arises: which women have been excluded — and do all those present really have a right to be there? This issue of inclusivity runs deep in the female psyche and fundamentally shapes the way women think and organise themselves. It is one of their major strengths, but, we must ask: what are its limits? Just as an untempered ethic of inclusivity and care for others once undermined women's position in family life, paralysing them in a forced — and false — choice between 'self-ishness' and 'caring for others', so it may now be doing the same in the broader political arena.

Traditionally in families, 'goodness' for women was equated with self-sacrifice and taking responsibility for others. In recent decades, women have become aware of the personal cost of such 'goodness' and have gradually won the right to include them-selves and their needs in the collective family bargaining. Women, with their almost instinctive pull towards renunciation of self and caring for others, have had to struggle to accept the essential notion of rights — that self-interest is legitimate and equal to the interests of others. It is now okay for women to think about themselves and to care for themselves in the context of family life.

But self-interest does not yet seem to be entirely legitimate for women in public life; it is not yet quite acceptable for individual women to acquire personal status. There is a slight sense of shame at the idea of achieving professional, vocational or polit-ical success relative to other women.

As more positions of power and influence become available to women, feminism is losing its innocence. Successful women increasingly find that they have to do battle with the romance of the women's movement, just as they once had to do battle with romantic, traditional notions of the family. As they begin to climb the ladder they were always supposed to climb, they find that they are being forced to challenge the assumption that it is more sisterly to struggle than to succeed; that 'good' feminists do not compete with other women; that conflict and status differentials with other women are wrong. The imminent prospect of varying levels of success for different women, of success for some women but not for others in particular arenas, will exacerbate this dilemma.

Women already know that if they are ever to acquire more power and influence, they have to engage with men and with the hierarchical worlds that men have created. They cannot afford to wait until the world is organised in a way that women find more congenial. As actual opportunities arise, women have to jump on a moving train. They have to learn the game of hierarchies, no matter how distasteful or boring they may find it. The long-term goal may still be the creation of a more woman-friendly and better world, but in the interim the existing world of men cannot be bypassed. The burden for many women at present is that, just as they are beginning to master the one-up/one-down dynamics of male hierarchies, they are obliged to honour a different set of reponsibilities related to the in/out dynamic of women's networks. As they jump on the moving train, it seems as if they are being asked again and again how many women, or how many women's issues, are they taking with them? Are they representing women properly? Which women? Whose interests are they including or excluding? The questions are, of course, entirely legitimate. But the tension created by the competing demands of the two worlds they inhabit — the women's world of collectivity-and-inclusion and the male world of hierarchies — often exhaust women who are newly involved in politics, trade unions, business and the media. The resulting burnout is a loss not only to the individuals concerned, but also to the broader movement towards equality.

Where does the womanly stance of collectivity and inclusion

originate psychologically? Why is it so central and persistent? We know from observations of children that this is an issue for girls from their earliest youth. Even in groups of preschool girls, tasks will be accomplished by all participating jointly in the decision-making. Girls tend to preface their proposals by saying 'Let's do this ... Let's ask her, shall we?' They talk in terms of 'we' rather than 'I'. In other words, they tend to see themselves, and to actually operate, as a community — as individuals engaged in a network of relationships. This is in contrast to preschool boys, who are already operating on a different set of assumptions: that life is a contest and that power and indeed enjoyment come from learning to act in opposition to others and insisting and resisting as a matter of principle. These fundamentally different ways of seeing and dealing with the world persist throughout childhood and into adulthood.

For girls, in a world conceived of as a community, intimacy is the key commodity to be bartered. The struggle is to stay in the centre of the network of relationships, the most secure and powerful position, and to avoid isolation and abandonment. Thus, the need is to minimise differences, to avoid conflict, to include everybody, to achieve consensus and to avoid at all costs being seen as superior (i.e. being 'bossy' or 'out for yourself'). Girls (and later women) operate on the assumption that, since they are a community, compliance with the group will increase the power of the group, not the individual power of the person involved. So when individual girls want to get their way, their strategy is to explain their actions as being for the common good, rather than personal preference ('Let's play in my house; it's nearer everybody'). Because of the collaborative way the invitation is framed, the other children who take it up will appear to be participating in the decision-making, rather than being told what to do.

The advantages of such an approach are considerable. When a wide range of people are consulted and involved in decision-making, they are more willing to implement the agreed policy because they feel that they have had a part in making it. But it also has its limitations. A conviction that they cannot and should not act alone can be a hindrance to women when they have to make quick or difficult decisions. An unwillingness to engage in conflict or confrontation poses a problem when women find themselves up against somebody determined to get their own way or somebody willing to exploit them. Such unwillingness to act alone ultimately will make it impossible to wield power.

The central ethic of the female notion of intimacy and community is: 'We are close and we are the same'. In such a world, assertion of status (i.e. difference) can be dangerous. Unless status is pursued in the guise of caring for others ('I'm not doing this for myself but for my children/all women') it carries with it the risk of being called selfish (i.e. abandoning others) and being isolated. Girls and women are extraordinarily sensitive to risks of this kind, and this heightened sensitivity can easily be exploited. It can act as a powerful form of social control of women by women, as well as of women by men.

The challenge now is to see whether bonds of mutuality and support can survive differential levels of success. Will the tension between individuality and collectivity simply overwhelm women already facing unequal odds? Most women want to keep faith with their characteristic way of organising themselves. They want to act in concert with other women, to ensure that the community of women, as well as themselves personally, grows stronger.

How can women learn a new etiquette of competition and conflict with each other which acknowledges the problem and allows for creative solutions? Can women, like men, learn to nurture collegiality through conflict?

If They Can Do It, Why Can't I?

Twenty-two women in the Dáil. Hmm. Dressed to kill and glittering with promise. There must be an awful lot of women around the country wondering 'If they can do it, why can't I?' But initial euphoria can quickly dissipate in the face of the usual dreary combination of male resistance, glass ceilings and women's own ambivalence. It is not so much that women give up the struggle for political power completely, as that they get stuck at a particular stage and cannot seem to move ahead.

One reason why individual women get stuck is that they resist making changes in their lives 'until they feel right about it'. They put off restarting their careers, or joining a political party, until all the circumstances are right. They store up their ambivalent feelings, waiting for a full and final internal resolution of their doubts and psychological conflicts about change. But very often, these conflicts cannot be resolved internally.

Instead, what is required is to actually begin to act, even in a small way. Limited plans can be tested in the real world, modified, then retried. Only by trying things out can you find out about your strengths and weaknesses. What psychologists have discovered is that behavioural change, however small, precedes changes in attitude and feeling. Your initial action will provide the impetus for you to change the set of beliefs and feelings that support your old way of doing things.

A common reason women do not put themselves forward publicly is their fear of being thought conceited and attention-seeking. They are afraid they will be isolated and lose the support of whatever network or group they depend on. Support from other women is sometimes based on the kind of solidarity that assumes 'we're all the same'. On the positive side, however, the very act of putting yourself forward will often flush out support from unexpected quarters. And the expected negative reaction is often not nearly as bad as you may have feared. Even when it is bad, the burst of courage needed to go forward in the first place creates a new kind of energy and strength. In the very process of trying out different things, new aspects of yourself become visible.

Feelings are the key. Many women regard feelings as their weak part, the bit that gets them into trouble. But feelings provide a constant barometer of all the information about the real world that you are constantly processing into your unconscious. Feelings can be made to work for you. This is especially true of negative feelings like fear, sadness and anger. Such feelings, instead of being viewed as unwanted intrusions, can be understood as a sign that something of critical importance to your welfare is under threat.

Feelings of anger are a sign that there has been a violation of your self, your territory or your values. Feeling angry can point to the need for protective solutions, such as setting limits on others' demands on you. Instead of wasting time thinking 'I should not feel this way', you should read the message behind your anger. Very often it will prompt you to take decisive action that may have been long overdue: 'This far, no farther'. Many women come to bitterly regret ignoring their anger and allowing themselves to be exploited.

Sadness, likewise, instead of being viewed as evidence that you cannot cope, can be interpreted as a cue for reparative solutions. If you understand your sadness as a sign that you need to compensate for some loss, it can energise you to seek out needed support, or to find a new field of endeavour in which to invest your talents.

What happens if you resist the call to action triggered by those negative feelings? The suppressed feelings will constantly threaten to surface. Many women feel that if they allow negative feelings any expression, they will be overwhelmed. 'If I start to cry, I will never stop ... If I get angry, I will leave the whole bloody lot of them behind me ...' They fear that their very selves will be destroyed. But the only self that will be lost is the one that has become used to her needs never being met; the self which has become too frightened to risk further disappointment.

For many women the most painful feeling that has to be faced is the fear that their lives have amounted to nothing, that they have not used their unique talents, that they are drifting — 'I have nothing to show at the end of the day'. Caught up in a cycle of responding to others' needs and others' expectations, they see no way of regaining control of their lives without risking being thought selfish or over-ambitious by themselves and others. While drifting may seem to offer safety, it carries with it the danger of a more painful confrontation with themselves later on. What was once simply a fear that they were not using their talents to the full, can turn into a conviction that they have no talents at all — no confidence, no nothing.

Their frustration and pent-up competitive energy may then find expression in resentment, bitterness and envy of other women. There are very few contexts, outside of psychotherapy, in which women can explore these 'politically incorrect' feelings. In the 1970s, women's consciousness-raising groups explored what it was like to live among powerful men. In the 1990s, living among other powerful women should be the focus. The need for an etiquette to deal with competitiveness and envy is a barely acknowledged problem among feminists.

Psychotherapy may seem a long way from politics, but the essence of psychotherapy is helping people to get unstuck, helping them to let go of ways of coping that were once effective but are no longer. We know from psychotherapy that the turning point often comes when a client is able to fully acknowledge her unmet needs: 'This is what I could have been, given half a chance.' It is only when individual women allow themselves to feel the full force of their own desires — to achieve in a personal way, to have status, to be in control, to shine — that they will release the energy that is needed to move forward socially and politically.

We also know from psychotherapy that the precursor to any change is the hope that things can be different. Without the expectation that change is possible, no action will be initiated, or the action attempted will be hesitant and tentative.

With twenty-two women in the Dáil, there is an air of hope.

But to be effective, hope must amount to more than a vague feeling of optimism. It must act as a kind of cognitive bridge between where you are now and where eventually you want to be. This does not require a master plan. For example, political 'reality' is very often fragmented and full of uncertainties. For women with political ambitions, hope simply means positioning themselves in a sufficient variety of promising places, with enough confidence to feel that they just might succeed. All that is required is that women's small successes all move in the same general direction, or at least all move away from some dismal present situation.

What militates against hope? Usually, it is a history of failure, of expectations not being met. Scepticism and inaction are then adopted as defensive manoeuvres to protect against further disappointments and to hide a sense of depression about oneself. But we know from research on depression that people often make unwarranted generalisations from one experience of failure to all others. The way to counter such generalisations is to analyse the specifics of each failure and to contain the failure within that particular set of circumstances.

It is also important to scrutinise the planned change for built-in preconceptions ('this is the way things always turn out ... there is only one way to solve this problem ... this is how people will react to me ...) see if these preconceptions can be modified, even slightly. Old attitudes cannot be abandoned immediately. All that is required is that they be set aside 'for now'.

What if you do not change, even though you have a good reason to? Then, there are emotional consequences. As a way of justifying what you turned down, you become more extreme in your original position. Your attitudes harden. But the conflict does not go away. After the next general election, you may still be left saying 'That could have been me ...'

If You're Not In, You Can't Win

About 50 per cent of Irish people now believe in women's right to equality in the home and in the workplace. Yet when individual women try to claim that equality — in politics, in business or in the home — they often face both external and internal resistence. Externally, they are confronted by structures and traditions that ignore them, attitudes that are antagonistic and networks of influence that exclude them. Internally, however, they have to contend with psychological upheavals which are equally dramatic and uncomfortable and which, if they are not managed properly, may subvert the external progress that is being made. As women begin to exercise real influence, they have to abandon old roles, as well as the psychological comforts and securities that went with these roles.

Can psychology offer any guidance about the best way to initiate and maintain change; how to combine effective external action with reasonable internal harmony and lack of stress? The answer is probably a qualified 'yes'. By examining the process of change in many different contexts, psychologists have identified a number of elements that seem to be consistently associated with success. While many of the specific recommendations are simply commonsensical, taken altogether they provide a useful perspective for anyone who is either planning long-term change or who wants to evaluate their own approach to it.

Thinking small

The first step is to select a goal that is small, specific, visible and attainable. You do not need any grand strategy. In fact, your initial goal may well be only loosely related to your final objective. How small is small? The guideline is that you should aim at either a major change in a relatively unimportant aspect of something; or a minor change in a relatively important aspect of something. The critical thing is that this first step is something you can build on, an action that signals, however modestly, that you are somebody to be reckoned with. By settling on a fairly circumscribed area of change and by separating this from the larger array of things that you are dissatisfied with, you have a much greater chance of maintaining control over both external events and your own internal fears and doubts.

The corrective emotional experience

In psychotherapy, what a person is most afraid to do, what he or she spends most effort avoiding, usually turns out to be the very thing they must do in order to solve their problems. Once they screw up the courage to act, they discover that the consequences they feared are not nearly as bad as they thought. The same logic applies to difficult or worrying changes in ordinary life. The trick is to scale down your initial goal so that your anxiety and doubts do not overwhelm you. But taking a real risk at some stage is an inevitable part of true change, and indeed to acknowledge that fact is itself liberating.

If you are successful, of course, it will boost your confidence. In addition, you may discover that a significant pocket of influence lies in an unexpected place, or that the feared backlash amounts to nothing more than a bit of huffing and puffing. Even if you are unsuccessful, you will often discover that the very process of taking action has released unexpected reserves of strength in yourself. Meanwhile, the next problem to be tackled has become clearer and it usually turns out to be different to what you thought it would be, because the first step has given you a new view of the world. For example, a woman who encounters sustained resistance to even the most minimal request for change may realise for the first time where the real power and control in a personal relationship or organisation rests. Such an insight is invaluable and may itself provide the impetus for further action.

Testing

The third step involves trying out the new behaviour in different contexts. Although you are still not entirely convinced that the successful outcome can be repeated ('I could just have been lucky'), you now have to test out the 'new you' more extensively. Having conquered your fear of speaking in public at the regular Parent-Teacher Association meeting, you must try it out at the annual general meeting, or put yourself forward for election to the committee. In retrospect, major changes may look as if there was a master plan all along (and, of course, successful people tend to promote this view of themselves), but the reality is that the steps involved in any one individual's success are usually fragmentary, and largely consist of identifying and taking up new opportunities as situations change.

Self-awareness

New behaviour is continually threatened by old patterns reasserting themselves, particularly in times of stress. To maintain the impetus of change, you need to develop an awareness of your own patterns of thought, and action is one way to do this. In psychotherapy, people are helped to become aware of the unconscious and repetitive patterns they adopt in their lives. Until they are aware of them, they cannot decide whether they want to continue these patterns or change them. In a more routine way, keeping a diary or journal can be surprisingly effective in uncovering patterns in your daily life which lead to success or failure in your new endeavours.

Finding a mentor, somebody who will guide you into the formal and informal culture of a political party, a trade union or a business organisation, is also a powerful way of developing awareness of how well or badly you are performing, how you are coming across. A mentor, somebody a woman completely trusts and knows is on her side, has been found to be a critical element in the success of women in large business corporations.

The just noticeable difference

People tend to be more interested in, and receptive to, new ideas that are just noticeably different to their own. Initial change which remains within this arena of the 'just noticeable difference' has the greatest chance of acceptance. To create change within these limits, however, requires subtlety and attention to detail. A woman's growing optimism that she can do something about a problem may get translated into agitation ('I'd better get going immediately') followed by an all-out assault or a dramatic gesture ('Let's get this done once and for all').

Dramatic gestures may frighten your opponents and create a forceful counterattack. For example, deciding to confront every vestige of sexism in an organisation all at once is likely to end in grief. Instead, at first try to be perceptibly unpredictable in how you respond to issues of gender. This is more likely to result in small wins in independence for you and correspondingly small losses, initially at least, for those colleagues who take you for granted. Since these small wins in independence are dispersed, they are also more difficult to attack.

Managing stress

Managing stress is crucial for change because high stress reduces one's problem-solving ability. Unmanageable stress comes from a fatal combination of three elements: big demands, an uncertain outcome, and a shaky perception of your own ability to cope. Women who want to enter the political arena may be able to do very little about the first two, but they can do something about the third.

This is where the strategy of starting off with compartmentalised, smaller problems pays off. The cost of failing is small ('This is no big deal'), the demands on you are reduced ('I just have this to do') and there is a perceived ability to cope ('I can do at least that'). Having done this much, you have an opportunity to rethink your view of yourself, to influence others' view of you, and to change your old patterns. In psychological terms, you gain insight. In political terms, you may one day become a government minister.

Waiting to be chosen?

Paradoxically, it is women's psychological strengths that often seem to hold them back in politics. Women are responsive, centred in the here-and-now of their lives, interested in self-development and in responding to others' needs. That is what makes them realistic, flexible, good at coping, ready to take up whatever opportunities they are offered.

But 'offered' is the key word. Women like to be asked, invited, noticed. They wait to be chosen. Head-hunting may bring some exceptional women into the party political system. In the long run, however, women must take the initiative themselves. If they want to enter politics, locally or nationally, they must talk directly to the people who matter. They must say what their goals are and what they are prepared to do to achieve them. It is not enough for women to be worthy and talented. They must be seen to be in the running.

Hungering to Win in the Diet Game

A woman colleague says to another, 'I'm starting my New Year's Resolutions next Monday'. Giving herself a little pinch she says, 'There's a bit of fat here I want to get rid of.' 'Yes,' the other sighs, 'Me too. I need to lose a few pounds as well.' It's not unlikely that this conversation was repeated thousands of times during the last few weeks and will continue to resonate, particularly in women's conversations for the rest of the year.

Exactly ten years ago, Judith Rodin, one of the leading psychologists researching eating and dieting, described women's worries about their weight to be 'a normative discontent'. In other words, if you are a woman it is now 'normal' to feel that you are overweight and to be more or less continuously preoccupied about shedding those few pounds. More than half of all women in western countries are, at any one time, on a diet. Moreover, concerns about dieting are poorly correlated with women's actual weight. It has been exhaustively established that while the ideal of female thinness has become more extreme, women are actually getting heavier. In the UK, for example, most women take a size bigger than 14.

More worryingly, there has been a rapid increase in the number of women being diagnosed as having eating disorders such as anorexia nervosa and bulimia. In fact, there is such an overlap between clinical populations of women with eating disorders and 'normal' women, in terms of their eating attitudes and behaviour, that it is sometimes not easy to draw a hard and fast line in that regard between what is 'normal' and what is 'abnormal'.

Scientists point out that most dieting (without long-term changes in eating and exercise patterns) is an expensive waste of time. Most weight loss is eventually regained. Worse, the weight lost, particularly on crash diets, tends to be of lean tissue and the weight regained tends to be fat. Crash diets set up a cycle of starvation/bingeing/further starvation. Body metabolism is altered so that resuming even normal eating will result in weight gain.

Why, in Rodin's words, do women pursue thinness like a career? Well, we know of course that they will suffer if they are fat. Being fat is highly stigmatised, for men and for women. Even very young children have a negative attitude to their chubby counterparts. Secondary school children prefer to keep a greater interpersonal distance from an obese classmate than from one with a handicap such as a missing hand or a facial disfigurement. The stigma is worse for women than for men. Some studies suggest that overweight women are less likely to get a third-level education and to be upwardly mobile than overweight men or their normal-weight female counterparts, though they do not differ from them on measures of intellectual ability and achievement.

There is evidence that for a woman, unlike a man, weight and body shape essentially determine whether she feels herself to be physically attractive. What she weighs can directly affect her self-esteem. 'I go on the scales nearly every morning,' a woman tells me. 'If I'm one or two pounds down, I'm on top of the world. I feel I can handle anything that day. If I'm up two pounds, I feel in despair. Why on earth am I spending my life fighting these two pounds?'

It is an unequal fight. Not only is a woman fighting her desire to eat food that is full of variety and choice, she is struggling to some degree against her body type and genes. Studies suggest that, on average, genes may be more powerful than environmental factors in determining weight. Identical twins reared apart end up with more similar weights than either non-identical twins or siblings reared together. The amount of overeating necessary to gain weight is far less for some people than for others. In a now classic study, it was shown that people's weight can remain stable, even though some were consuming far more calories than others (ranging from 1,600 to 7,400 per day) — and that was allowing for gender, age, and activity level.

Women are genetically predisposed to have a higher

proportion of fat to lean tissue than males. For example, a critical amount of fat is necessary to start and maintain the menstrual cycle. Moreover, at each major hormonal milestone in a woman's life — puberty, pregnancy and menopause — the changes in a woman's body can produce rapid fluctuations in weight regulation systems. Susan Brownmiller's study of what constitutes 'femininity' suggests that female fat has always presented a dilemma. Fat creates the desired curves, but it is also bulky. Bulky means big, and big means masculine. Hence, in their efforts to define and present themselves as feminine, women have always been preoccupied with the amount of flesh that has been considered desirable and have expended great effort and ingenuity in finding ways to contain, rearrange, mould, highlight and reduce it.

Understood in that context, dieting could be seen as the modern equivalent of the corset or two-way elastic, only now, instead of relying on external support, women have to restrict all the wobbly bits themselves. The parallel between dieting and corsets goes beyond this. Corsets did not just improve the figure, they had moral significance as well. Women were prepared to endure considerable discomfort and, in the case of corsets, danger to their health, to contain all the soft fleshiness that might embarrass a woman by suggesting looseness, wantonness, indiscreet sexuality, lack of self-discipline. Corsets armoured women, making them feel firmly held and secure, disciplined and respectable, women of standing. Dieting and thinness do the same.

But who sets the physical ideal for women? The traditional feminist view is that male values are the culprit. These arguments are so well known, they need no repeating. Yet, though women may say they diet to please men, this does not appear to be the only or even the most important reason. In fact, studies show that the ideal figure aspired to by women is significantly thinner than men would actually like. (Interestingly, the male figure which men believe is most attractive to women is actually a lot bigger than women would prefer. So both sexes are misinformed about what the other finds attractive.)

Brownmiller concedes that physical appearance remains the most intense form of female-to-female competition. The pursuit of thinness may simply be the current weapon in this peculiar form of refined physical struggle. Women know that this is an achievement that is highly visible and its significance will be understood across social, generational and class barriers.

Any woman who has witnessed that moment of pure triumph when a successful dieter parades her new figure in front of other women will understand this. The whinnies of admiration, the unstinted praise for the moral courage and determination shown, the sighs of envy, the awed silence as the woman recounts how she did it — these constitute for most women the equivalent of winning the Prix de France or the Person of the Year Award.

While men may put all their effort into achieving and maintaining a one-up position in the various hierarchies in their lives, women are expending considerable energy in the pursuit of physical perfection and in assessing how they are doing in relation to other women. This is why, when many women enter a room, they automatically sweep their gaze over the other women there and rank themselves in the quintessential female hierarchy: who is thinner, who is fatter. In fact, women who are highly ambitious and successful in their work, who have high and perfectionist standards for personal performance, tend to be more dissatisfied with their own bodies and feel fatter —regardless of their actual weight — than less ambitious women.

But what is wrong with such competition you might ask, apart from the endless titivating, tears and tantrums about every little physical imperfection? The tumble is, female competition, like male competition, can easily become excessive and self-destructive. It can take up an inordinate amount of time and effort. Dieting, like all beautification routines, can concentrate women's minds on every detail of what they eat, what they weigh, what they measure. In their never-ending quest for self-perfection, many women are never free from self-consciousness, never quite happy with themselves, easily undermined by remarks (real or imagined) about their appearance. Women, it turns out, no less than men, are vulnerable to the compulsive nature of competition.

There have been attempts, largely unsuccessful, to make fat a feminist issue. But women persist in keeping their physical appearance, particularly their weight, to the forefront of their definition of self-worth, happiness and success as women. That is why talking 'objectively' about diets and dieting largely misses the point, unless it is acknowledged that dieting has become a way for women to define how well they are doing as women, in relation to some primitive standard of femininity. Women have little patience with men's devotion to what they regard as an out-moded standard of masculinity. Is it not time that our often unconscious standards of femininity were also reviewed?

Mum's the Word

'A son is a son till he gets him a wife, a daughter is a daughter for the rest of her life.'

Twenty years of psychological research has established that the great majority of mothers and daughters describe the relationship between them as intimate, enduring and psychologically rewarding. Throughout the lifespan, this relationship stays warm and supportive, often characterised by a pattern of mutual mothering. But regular periods of conflict, tension and ambivalence are also reported. What serpent intrudes on this potential paradise of closeness between mothers and their daughters?

Interestingly, it is daughters who report the most conflict. They also feel that their mothers win most arguments. Their mothers, on the other hand, think the same conflicts are less significant, and they report that the problems are most often solved 'by compromise'. These findings suggest a number of interesting things about mothers and daughters. First, daughters perceive more conflict in the relationship because it is their task to psychologically separate and become independent. They have more reason to be vigilant about their mother's intrusions. Second, the power and dependency balance of childhood is renegotiated in adulthood, with ageing mothers gradually becoming more dependent on their daughters, and therefore increasingly ready to deny any potential rift between them.

Of course, the very intimacy of the relationship creates a potential for irritation. Mothers and their adult daughters know an extraordinary amount about each other. In their conversations, mothers recount every detail of their daily diet, every ache and pain, every item of gossip about neighbours and friends.

Verbatim accounts of third-party conversations are relayed, amid painstaking enquiry about the daughter's children, health, weight, household news, clothes, and sometimes work. For the most part, mothers supply and demand more detail, the detail serving as a way of bonding the relationship with the daughter and keeping it close. Enquiry-and-account become a currency of caring. Talking for only fifteen minutes is considered by some mothers to be 'rushing off the phone'.

The problem, of course, is that, since maintaining closeness and connection is the primary goal, conflicts between mothers and their adult daughters can be characterised by a certain indirectness and obfuscation. Mothers find it hard to give up their old, dominant role. Battles of will are obscured by a rhetoric of care and collaboration, and the mother's liberal use of the word 'we'. Daughters, edgy about their autonomy, try to stick resolutely to the word 'I'.

(*Mother:* 'Let's do this, shall we? We'd really enjoy that.
Daughter: Well, you might enjoy it, Mum, but I'm not sure I would.
Mother: Ah, we'll enjoy it alright.')

Mother makes seemingly innocent requests or enquiries ('Is there any chance you could do this for me? Only if you can, of course.') Daughter resists and only the ensuing coldness and flurry of hurt feelings make clear that the apparent invitation was really a command or demand. If, however, the daughter accuses her mother of sulking, further complications arise. ('What do you mean why am I angry? I'm not angry. I only said I wondered why you were in such bad humour.') In fact 'I only said ...', the symbol par excellence of indirect female communication, reaches a kind of perfection in mother-daughter discourse, managing simultaneously to convey hurt, denial and criticism, as well as a claim for further clarification and negotiation.

Small wonder, then, that things get fraught with tension at times. Of course, there are moments when the adult daughter thinks she has the problem licked. Free, free, free at last! But mothers do not give up easily. They keep coming back to disagreements. They want to sort things out, remake connections, restore the old intimacy. But they also like to have their own way. Just as peace is almost restored, there is a final volley. 'I still think you should have done what I suggested. But I'll say no more ...' Game, set and match to mother.

This is why grown women, in full control of their work and homes, are sometimes reduced to wails of outraged self pity by their mothers. Yet, the most they can manage in the way of emotional catharsis is to hiss 'I hate my mother'. This, of course, is usually delivered well out of the mother's hearing, followed by a torrent of sobs and hastily cut short by penal guilt.

Men are mystified by all this emotion. 'Why', they ask, 'do you take such notice of her? If she is that impossible, why have so much to do with her? What do you care what she thinks of you?'

'Ah, you don't understand at all', their women snap, going out to telephone their sisters or women friends — who will understand only too well the primitive emotion that flows between mothers and daughters.

Of course, there are impeccable psychological reasons for this intensity. The first and most fundamental emotional attachment is with your mother. A mother is every infant's first love, first witness, first boss, the first representative of the world. This is true for both sons and daughters. But to develop a male identity, a son has to psychologically separate from his mother and identify with his father. A daughter does not have to make that break. She will learn her female identity from her mother and this does not contradict her primary sense of oneness and attachment with her mother. For a girl, the twin engines of identification and attachment chug along together. Thus, girls grow up with a sense of continuity and similarity to their mother, a relational connection to the world.

This process of identification and closeness is mutual. Although sons and daughters were originally part of her body, a mother often consciously and unconsciously experiences her son as more 'other' than her daughter. There is a more profound sense of identity and continuity with her daughter, often experienced immediately after the birth. 'When I looked at her,' one mother said, 'I thought "some day you will go through this very experience" and I had such a rush of feelings towards her.' As she watches her daughter grow, a mother feels the burden of being the role model for her. Women who hitherto have endured oppressive and damaging relationships, or have been unable to express or use their talents, can often, for the first time, find the personal strength to improve their situation by saying to themselves, 'Whatever about myself, I owe it to my daughter to do better than this. I must lead the way for her.'

The result of this close identification is that mothers and daughters develop an often extraordinary empathy for each other. They can partake of each other's feelings, often knowing intuitively how things are for the other. There is great subtlety in their caring and stroking. At best, each knows the other 'is always there for me'. There is a sense of mutual responsibility and protectiveness. When it works, it is love of a high order.

At worst, this sense of continuity and similarity can blur psychological boundaries. While the mother has little to lose by an excess of intimacy, the daughter, who still has to achieve her own identity, is in danger of being swamped, enmeshed, becoming an extension of her mother. She may never emerge or be allowed to emerge as a separate person, with clear boundaries around herself. She can develop life-long problems in regulating closeness in all relationships.

Time and time again in the psychological research on women, 'Relationship with own mother' turns out to be critical in understanding how women cope with the major tasks in their lives. For example, when women become mothers for the first time, the way they bond with their babies, how they feel about themselves, their sense of mastery and their sense of pleasure, are all significantly affected by how they feel about their mothers.

For daughters, the pull towards the mother is very powerful. From her they learn what it means to be female; from her they learn what love and nurturing mean. The lessons learned may be inadequate, the daughter may strenuously disagree with her mother's interpretations, but it is against her mother's version that she must rebel. Positively or negatively she must model herself on her mother. Mothers have to act as the beginner's kit for their daughter's identity.

For women, the central core of self seem to be organised and developed around their capacity to be competent in relationships. The critical component of that emotional competence is the capacity for empathy — that is, the ability to experience, understand and respond to the inner state of another person. Girls look primarily to their mother to teach them this very complex set of skills.

That is why little girls like to be physically close to their mother, to be part of her world. They scan her face for signs of her feelings and sense the slightest change in her mood. An intuitive understanding flows between them. 'Are you alright, Mummy? Why are you sad?' a young daughter will ask, often before anybody else has sensed her mother's mood. Girls like occasionally to mother their mother, to practice the art of nurturing, as long as they can return to being children when they need to. If they are not allowed that closeness, they feel pushed away, denied, not well understood. They may not be able to articulate it, but they may also begin to feel incompetent, inferior. Although her mother may encourage other abilities, unless she also validates her ability to be loved and to love, her daughter's core sense of self and of self-esteem will remain fragile and easily shaken.

Little boys like to be close to their mother too. But because of their different needs, they are more vigilant about their sense of separateness. They gleefully revel in their power to shut out the mother's voice. Boys are always pulling away, unwilling to be bound or controlled by their mother's feelings. For a girl, more attentive to and interested in emotional sharing with their mothers, the major psychological issue is to regulate the closeness of her relationship with her mother while at the same time defining her own identity in relation to her. All that is special and potentially destructive about the mother-daughter relationship flows from how that balance is achieved. Most serious conflicts in the mother-daughter relationship stem originally from the mother's denial of her daughter's need for closeness or for autonomy.

For example, closeness may be impossible if a mother is beset by rivalrous feelings about her daughter. The dynamics between them, whose theme is 'We care about each other', becomes distorted into a competitive 'Who needs care the most?' The mother can never take the nurturing role, always experiencing her own needs as more urgent than anybody else's. Very often, such mothers were themselves rejected by their own mothers and project on to their daughters all their own fierce resentment and bitterness about not being nurtured themselves. The daughter becomes the 'bad girl', the unloved daughter-part of the mother. Though they themselves experienced the pain of neglect and rejection, they repeat history with their daughters. They shut out the daughter's pain because it reminds them too much of their unacknowledged pain in relation to their own mothers.

Such competition may cause the daughter to turn to her father for succour. Most times, a daughter will look to the father for that primary attachment only if the mother fails her, shuts her out. If the mother's self-esteem is low, she may even misinterpret her daughter's normal attachment to her father as 'leaving her', rejecting her, further inflaming her rivalry with her daughter.

An equally serious, but much less obvious, problem may arise when a daughter is not accorded a fully separate self by her mother. A too powerful and needy mother may incorporate the daughter, seeing her as an extension of herself. She constantly tells her: 'You are just like me in every way' or 'I know just what you are thinking'. Not being treated as a separate person is difficult for the daughter to identify as a problem since such overpowering mothers are often affectionate and indulgent in many respects. What is hard for a child to detect is that the indulgence is tied much more to the mother's mood than the daughter's need and often masks wilfulness, intrusiveness and domination. Such a mother demands that her daughter mirrors her feelings. When she feels bad, she finds it an affront if her daughter does not feel bad too. If she is buoyed up, she becomes outraged if the daughter will not share her happiness. She constantly intrudes on her daughter's space, physical and psychological, blurring the boundary between her own and her daughter's reality. A mother who sees her daughter as an extension of herself gradually will render the daughter incapable of knowing whose feelings belong to whom. The normal process of empathy, that is, participating in the feelings of another, becomes distorted into actually experiencing the feelings of another as one's own.

Seduced by this overidentification with her mother, the daughter cannot develop strong boundaries around herself and that sense of confident separateness that is the basis of self-esteem and mastery. Her capacity to feel for her mother can easily become a crippling proneness to guilt, particularly if her mother is unhappy or unfulfilled. Unconsciously, the daughter may feel that she has no right to happiness unless she can first make her mother happy. She may feel that she has no right to her own possessions, place, opinions or feelings. Worse, she may unconsciously carry all those habits into her adult intimate relationship.

How can such mother-daughter relationships be improved in adult life? The challenge for the daughter is to change both her inner and outer relationship with her mother. For many women, the transforming experience is to learn (often for the first time) to set limits with their mothers, to be able to say 'no' without feeling overwhelmed by guilt. But that step is possible only if the daughter can also challenge and, if necessary relinquish, the image of herself that came from her mother. What many women find out is that the price they paid for closeness with their mothers is to internalise an image of themselves that significantly restricts the range of feelings they can express or rights they can claim.

To reclaim herself, a daughter has to learn to 'foster-mother' herself; that is, to internalise an attentive, listening, caring relationship to herself. Only in that way will she gradually learn to feel 'real', connected and purposeful in her relationships and thereby develop a new, more balanced understanding of herself and her mother. The goal, eventually, is to be able to say, with a measure of calm acceptance: 'My mother's way of doing things is not for me, but as a person she is OK. I understand why she had the faults she had and why I have the faults I do.' With that realisation, daughters walk down the long path to wisdom: the awareness that looking for perfection in your mother is another version of looking for perfection in yourself, and when you finally forgive yourself, you forgive your mother.

How's Your Father?

What do children think of their fathers?

'You have more fun with dads. They play with you and take you places and buy you treats ... Mums deal with the emotional side of your life. They put more meaning into things, like they tell you how people will feel about things. Dads are better at telling you about image problems — like being popular or being bullied — things that embarrass boys ... It's harder to get a Dad's love. You have to work harder to get him to praise you or say "I love you" though I know he does ...'

'Mums are boss of the home. They make the rules. But Dads enforce them. Dads get more ratty. They suddenly get annoyed and roar. Mums get upset and pile up all the things they did for you and say "You've really upset me".'

'Fathers get girls to act more feminine. They let girls be more temperamental. They expect girls to do more for them at home. They know that if they asked, a girl would do it, but that a boy would argue. They know girls are more dedicated.'

'Dads are more interested in what you look like ... Dads make you act more like a boy. They say "Act like a big boy, grow up, stop messing", though they usually say it only once a year. Fathers like boys to be popular and good at sports; not to mind losing. They like a boy to be like themselves, you know, not girly. Mothers don't mind if you are

in between because they are ladies themselves. Mums are
more caring. But Dads tell you about the world.'

The above are a selection of comments about fathers which I
elicited from an admittedly small sample of children. They reflect
many of the historically disparate images of fatherhood that
shape the role itself: mediator between the family and the larger
world; rule-enforcing patriarch; guardian of sex roles; playmate.
Fathers, the psychoanalysts used to say, love dangerously. Their
love is contingent on performance of one kind or another.

Mothers love in quite a different way, non-contingently. They
love you for yourself, more expressively and openly. Consequently, when mothers love you or do not love you, it goes to
the core of your being. When fathers love or do not love you,
you may not know it for certain until you are grown up.
Psychologists studying women who were highly successful in
their careers found that a warm, involved relationship with their
fathers was an almost universal characteristic. There is also the
negative effects. Many of the crises of confidence experienced by
men, the problems of career stagnation and early burn-out, can
be traced to undermining, competitive fathers in childhood, to
fathers who could not bear the idea that their sons would out-
strip them in any field.

Fathering seems to remain curiously invisible, a black box, to
fathers themselves. If you ask men what makes for a good father,
they look puzzled, scratch their heads, shuffle their feet. Then
light dawns: 'Being a good provider' they say, momentarily
relieved. 'Bringing home the bacon'. But almost immediately
they wonder just how important they are in the actual day-to-
day lives of their children.

Are modern fathers capable, then, of becoming more like
mothers? A resounding 'Yes' from the research. Fathers can
soothe, stimulate, nurture and baby-talk babies as well as
mothers. The only problem is that by and large they do not.
Researchers in home observation studies find that the new, sensitive and nurturant fathers are often 'reading', 'watching television' or just plain 'out'. But this does not mean that their role
as parents is unimportant. By far the most interesting modern

research suggests that it is in and through their relationship with the mother that fathers play a crucial role in determining the quality of mothering which children receive.

We know that even women from extremely deprived and unhappy backgrounds can become competent and responsive mothers if they have a supportive husband. We also know that stress can seriously interfere with good mothering and that the most frequently reported stresses in women's lives relate to marital problems. Moreover, we know that fathers' direct involvement with their children is yoked to how well they are getting on with their wives. We know very little, however, about what specific support husbands need from their wives in order to make good fathering possible.

The problem of defining what fathers are and do is inextricably bound up with the problem of defining masculinity. Men have some vague sense that they should be instilling and passing on the ancient male values of heroism, competitiveness, physical prowess and bravery in protecting women, children and territory. The male imagination (if we are to judge from surveys of their preferences in reading material) is still captivated by fantasies of high adventure, overcoming danger and mastering nature. Admittedly, the average suburban father, feeling like a domestic Hercules in chains, has to content himself with pottering around with power tools, putting up the holiday tent and being authoritative about the car. But it does not take from the fact that in their secret heart most men want to be heroes — at least in the eyes of their women and children.

Fortunately, the modern father has been partly rescued by sport. Sport, in the absence of war, provides a cultural stage for male heroism, that peculiar mix of performance, display and courage. Dads can bring their sons to junior sports fixtures and yell 'Keep 'em under pressure', secure in the knowledge that they are fulfilling a fatherly role (though mothers are in here too).

It was simpler in the days when fathers were patriarchs, with land and money and jealously guarded skills to hand on; a certain amount of filial piety was guaranteed. Any additional role-scripting was supplied by Freud, who gave fathers a starring role in the oedipal drama.

According to Freud, the little boy automatically forms a deep and erotic attachment to his mother, but fears unconsciously that he will draw on himself his father's jealousy and vengeance. For a boy, the ultimate threat is castration by his father. This puts paid to his oedipal longings. He gives up his mother, identifies with his father and thereby joins the society of men. This successful oedipal resolution becomes the bedrock of his conscience and his male desire for mastery and achievement.

One enduring element of the modern father's role is a kind of anxious vigilance for any hint of feminine tendencies in sons. Psychologists have catalogued fathers' (usually covert) attempts to exert sex-role pressure on boys in particular. One father, when asked by a researcher if he would be upset by signs of femininity in his son, replied: 'Yes, I would be. Very, very much. Terrifically disturbed — couldn't tell you the extent of my disturbance.'

But it would be simple-minded to think of fathers as just promoting machismo. The research indicates that boys reared without fathers may become stereotypically masculine — fighting and getting into trouble at an early age. Paradoxically, then, the presence of a father seems actually to tone down excesses in the definition of the male sex role.

Fathers have also experienced rapid cultural change in how they are expected to parent their daughters. In the old Freudian doctrine, daughters, discovering that, alas, they had no penis, had to give up all hope of becoming powerful like Daddy, and had to settle instead for falling in love with him. The hope and promise was that if the daughter identified with her mother, and grew up like her, she too could have her own man and her own babies. The father's role was to encourage little girls to be feminine. Dr Spock, in the 1957 edition of *Baby and Child Care*, suggested practical guidelines: 'I'm thinking of the little things he [the father] can do, like complimenting her on her dress, or hair-do, or the cookies she's made.'

The modern father, negotiating the new danger zone of sexism, is circumspect about how he frames compliments to his daughter. Yet, we all know intuitively that girls need affirmation of their sexual identity and role from the man they know and love the best, their father. One study showed, for example, that daughters of widows may become unusually shy and withdrawn; and that girls whose parents separate may become prematurely interested in sexual relationships and be insecure and inappropriately seductive with men. And there is yet another tension for men. With the growing awareness of child sexual abuse, many loving and affectionate fathers are now less secure about showing physical affection to their daughters.

In many families, the main drama seems to lie in the father-son relationship and the psychological salience of the father in ushering his adolescent son to manhood. Our children force us to be heroes. 'A boy wants something very special from his father', wrote Sherwood Anderson. 'When I was with other small boys and he passed along the street, I wanted to feel in my breast the glow of pride. "There he is. That is my father".'

Fathers will look in vain for an inspiring Christian image of the good father, riveted as we are by the cultural icon of Madonna and child (with St Joseph safely boxed in as 'The Worker'). In psychological terms, perhaps St Christopher, with the child securely aloft on his shoulders, captures more accurately the nature of fatherhood: the child both a heavy responsibility and the giver of meaning to his father's own journey.

But to become a man, every son ultimately needs to struggle with his father — the protagonist of the old order — to metaphorically slay the dragon, and to become himself the hero, the champion of the new. It is a struggle, however, which must be tempered by love, and is only possible through love. Because the old order has to be first taught by a beloved father.

One of Freud's own most fervent adolescent wishes was to stand one day on the Acropolis. Nevertheless, when he eventually fulfilled that desire, his triumph was mixed with an unexpected depression. It produced one of his great insights into the psychology of father-son relationships: 'It must be that a sense of guilt was attached to the satisfaction in having got so far: there was something about it that was wrong, that was from the earliest times forbidden ... It seems as though the essence of success were to have got further than one's father.'

That peculiar, poignant longing that sons have for their fathers' acknowledgment and forgiveness has also been a great theme of many Irish writers — Synge, Murphy, McGahern, Friel, Leonard and, of course, Joyce. The last sentence of *A Portrait of an Artist as a Young Man* still resonates: 'Old father, old artificer, stand me now and ever in good stead.'

A Crisis of Sexuality in the Church

Freud never underestimated the power of sexual desire, its risky, unstable, subversive potential. Unattended sexual desire can disrupt the most orderly lives and, as we now know, the most ordered institutions. Freud argued that 'the psychical value of sexual satisfaction increases with its frustration. The dammed-up libido is now put in a position to detect one or other of the weaker spots which are seldom absent in the structure of sexual life, and there to break through and obtain satisfaction of a neurotic kind in the form of pathological symptoms.'

A torrent of sexual scandals has hit the Catholic Church and it looks at times as if the moral authority of the Church, its traditional power to heal and console, may also be swept away. For many, the defining moment in this growing crisis was the morning we heard about Bishop Casey and Annie Murphy. But, as one priest ruefully told me this week, the bishop's affair is beginning to sound less shocking, even innocent, in the context of the more recent revelations about paedophile priests.

In the heated debate about the Church's sexual teachings, the sexuality — or rather the non-sexuality — of the clergy was, up to now, a given. Whatever about taming the unruly desires of its flock and the fertility of women, it was assumed that priests at least had resolved the issue of their own sexual life by their commitment to celibacy. It now seems that the hierarchy is hoping that the recent evidence to the contrary can be explained away by the bad apple theory that these are isolated 'sexual acts', transgressions by weak individuals, sins, which can be confessed, forgiven, sent away.

What the Church is not facing up to is that such 'acts' are a reflection of deeply unresolved issues in its own teaching about sexuality and of the aura of denial, secrecy and rationalisation that surrounds the sexuality of the clergy. These interlocking themes are taken up by theologian William M. Shea, who describes the 'tangle of issues' that the Catholic Church has failed to deal with credibly. These issues all have to do with sexuality.

> They are: family life, divorce and remarriage, premarital and extramarital sex, birth control, abortion, homosexuality, masturbation, the role of women in ministry, their ordination to the priesthood, the celibacy of the clergy, and the male monopoly of leadership. Some have suggested that sex is, at bottom, the issue that clogs up our Catholic calendar. Fear of women, and perhaps hatred of them, may well be just what we have to work out of the Catholic system.

For the Church, these issues constitute a seamless fabric — the rationale being that to remove one strand would weaken the whole fabric of its authority on sexual matters. Yet if the Church is to retain moral credibility in relation to any of those matters, it has to be prepared to engage in a real discourse about the biological, psychological and social realities of sexuality in the modern world, instead of clinging to increasingly irrelevant pronouncements about what is good, bad and unmentionable.

The sexual revolution, particularly the development of effective contraception, and the growth of the women's and gay rights' movements, have left the Church stranded with an archaic psychology of sexuality, increasingly at variance with the experience of ordinary people. The world has moved away from a view of sex as simply procreation, as exclusively an 'act' of heterosexual intercourse involving modest foreplay, penetration and 'satisfaction'. What also preoccupies men and women now is trying to understand the psychological roots and branches of their own sexuality: how it was formed, how central it is to their self-esteem and identity and, probably most essentially, how it makes and breaks their relationships.

Very few are looking to the Church for guidance in this field. And why would they? After all, the Church's teaching on sexuality continues to insist that all directly sought sexual pleasure (thought, word, desire or action) outside marriage is gravely sinful, and that every act of sexual intercourse within marriage must remain open to the transmission of life. The present pope insists that sexual intercourse, even within marriage, is not only 'incomplete', but even ceases to be an act of love if contraception is used. Do the vast majority of people — celibate or non-celibate, clergy or faithful — actually believe this? Such pronouncements are so much at variance with the experience of most people as to seriously undermine the Church's credibility in the arena of intimate relationships. The faithful have learned to find their own solutions to their psychological and sexual dilemmas. Even members of the clergy, when they are troubled by their own sexual problems, do not seem to turn to each other for help, except in the confessional.

Richard Sipe, a priest now retired from the active ministry, has concluded, on the basis of his research in the United States, that a significant minority of priests are not celibate — or only intermittently so. He estimates that about 20 per cent of priests are, at any one time, involved in a more or less stable sexual relationship with a woman or with sequential women in an identifiable pattern of behaviour. An additional 8 to 10 per cent are involved in exploratory 'dating type' relationships that may include incidental sexual contacts. These transient sexual relationships often seem to serve as a 'prove myself' experience for the priest as part of his attempt to bridge the gap between whatever adolescent sexual experiences he may have had and his present adult relationships, or even to prove to himself that he is indeed committed to celibacy.

Some of the remaining 70 per cent try to solve the problem of their loneliness by asking women to become close companions — to have an intimate relationship that does not include sex. But often priests in this situation come to discover how dependent their celibacy is on the traditional all-male clerical structure of their lives. For example, in recent years, when priests were allowed more freedom of movement and the traditional institutional structures in their lives weakened, their inherent emotional and sexual immaturity was often revealed by their behaviour in relationships with women. Women in such relationships with priests were often exploited, used as a vehicle for the priest's 'growth', providing an experience that was rationalised as sending him back 'as a better priest'.

Richard Sipe's research also suggests that approximately 10 per cent of clergy in the United States involve themselves in homosexual activity. If those who identify themselves as homosexual or at least have serious questions about their sexual orientation are included, the proportion can go up to 22 per cent — though of course not all these priests are sexually active. These men find themselves in a Church which views a homosexual orientation as 'an objective disorder', 'a more or less strong tendency towards moral evil'. They also find themselves in a Church that has a strong homosocial organisation — that is where men are central and submissive to a male hierarchical authority and where women are incidental and dispensable. How can homosexual men, or those troubled by their orientation, work out their sexual identity in such an environment?

It is hardly surprising, then, that real and serious problems such as paedophilia are also denied or are shrouded in secrecy. It should be remembered that only about 2 per cent of Catholic priests are paedophiles (though an additional 4 per cent are preoccupied to some extent with adolescent boys and girls and may sometimes act on these fantasies). Richard Sipe describes the traditional way the Church has dealt or failed to deal with this problem: remonstration with the erring priest, sending him on religious retreat, or assigning him to another parish. Throughout the 1980s the Church in the US learned at great cost that a different response was needed. Was the Irish hierarchy not alerted by the experience in the US to the inadequacy of the traditional response to the problem of paedophilia among priests?

In the wake of the current sexual scandals, many priests feel obliged to reassure their families that they are not gay, paedophile, and are not having affairs with women or fathering children. The ordinary foot-soldiers of the Church, who have adhered to a celibacy that puts the extraordinary energy of their sublimated sexuality at the disposal of the community, must be deeply wounded by the current scandals. Do they feel supported by the Church? Do they think it was worth it?

Celibacy is not just sexual abstinence. Rather, it is one way to come to terms with one's sexual energies. But it cannot be achieved without confronting one's own sexuality. The Church urgently needs to know how priests and religious women are faring in that struggle. Nobody wants to lose the crucial, reassuring moral presence that the priest and the religious represent in Ireland. Their brand of committed, intelligent altruism constitutes a large part of what we Irish call our 'quality of life'. But they must learn to include themselves, to join the rest of us in a more equal, compassionate discourse on sexuality. Only then will there be any possibility of a truly grown-up doctrine of sexuality.

Wishful and Magical Thinking

Christmas is upon us. The season has unfolded in the time-hon-oured way: four parts hype, three parts goodwill, two parts excess and one part panic. Each individual and family are, of course, constitutionally free to vary the recipe according to their own lights. Some specialise in excess, others in panic, a few *artistes* bringing both to an exquisite pitch. By now, the number of shop-ping days has finally run out. Surrounded by bands of frantic people still dithering existentially at the perfume counter or sigh-ing behind you at the check-out, you may be asking, not for the first time, what it is all for. You are not alone. All over the free world, millions of others are wondering exactly the same thing.

Every year there are prophets warning us that Christmas has got too big. The ads on television, the pressure to spend, the greed, the gluttony, the absence of 'the real spirit of Christmas' are all ritually denounced. This 'real spirit of Christmas' is invariably conjured up in memories of past Christmases. It is always located a tantalising one generation back, in some half-remembered personal or historical past.

This longing for Christmas past is as much part of the season as presents and pudding. We all yearn for the golden age of childhood when Santa Claus read our secret desires and we could wake on Christmas morning to find that our wishes had been granted. We remember the confident feeling that it was good to be a child, that the season was ours, that once a year at least we got our heart's delight. And all we had to do was wait and nourish that exquisite sense of anticipation. Those who loved us made it happen.

There is something so deeply captivating about that experi-ence that we never really leave it behind; no more than we can ever fully get over the unforgettable desolation of blighted Christmases when adults failed us in those awful dramas of domestic pain that were ritually re-enacted.

The psychological meaning of Christmas is deeply rooted in the unconscious. Christmas happens at the darkest, most barren time of the year. The Christian church decided to commemorate the unknown date of the birth of Christ at the ancient time of the winter solstice, when our ancestors lit huge bonfires to encourage the sun to warm the earth and make it fruitful again, thus uniting symbolically the birth of a new era with the reawakening of the earth each spring. In a world of uncertainty and anxiety, we have to borrow strength from the power of magic. What, asks psychoanalyst Bruno Bettelheim, could hold more magic for us than the promise of a new beginning, the rebirth of the world, the birth of a child? It is easy to see why Christmas is especially a feast for children, because they are our most profound investment in the future, the way we are all reborn.

How we try to make Christmas special for children reveals our unconscious knowledge of what, at least occasionally, we all need, children most of all. The child becomes the centre of affectionate attention, the focus of generosity and indulgence, the nexus around which the family groups. The entire family and community collude in trying to create for the child a world that corresponds to his or her wishful and magical thinking. In the figure of Santa Claus, there is the embodiment of somebody all powerful yet full of goodwill, able to indulge every child in the world, yet knowing the special heart's desire of each single one. Through Santa, the child feels part of the great fellowship of children, yet singled out in the most delightful way. Santa excites no envy or jealousy because he conveys in those early vital years of childhood the promise of a benevolent and gratifying world, the security of abundance, the utter joy of unconditional love.

The child who experiences that yearly outpouring of love and goodwill is buttressed in a profound way against future adversity. At the psychologically darkest moments, he or she can reach back consciously and unconsciously to that fund of memories and draw psychological sustenance from them. Bettelheim tells the story of a group of child refugees who had to escape from

Norway after the Nazi invasion. They had to flee in deep winter over the high mountains into Sweden, taking only what they could carry on their backs. They had to leave behind all their worldly possessions, taking only what was necessary for survival. The group took its first desperate rest after reaching the safety of the Swedish border. When they had eaten the small amount of food they had taken along, there was little left in the children's small knapsacks.

When the group leader happened to look into one child's bag, he found there, among the pitiful few objects, a small silver star for a Christmas tree. The other children had packed similar keepsakes: cheap Christmas decorations, stars and bells, bits of tinsel and glitter. They had taken along these ornaments, Bettelheim says, as symbols of the happiness they had once known with their families, and also as symbols of the higher, magical power of Christmas. It was as if these objects alone could cast a spell of safety over their loneliness, impotence and uncertain future. But most of all, these tokens of Christmas represented a promise that the happiness that was once theirs would be theirs again.

But what of those children whose Christmases were blighted? For them, as adults, the season brings a yearly return of depression, desolation and anxiety. Sometimes these anniversary reactions are conscious. The lead up to Christmas is full of dread and worry. It went wrong all the other times, why should it go right now? Masters of the pre-emptive strike, they settle for cynicism, self-protection and defensiveness — anything that will prevent them from again feeling the unbearable pain of disappointment.

Others have buried their pain so deep that they have no real awareness why they experience such irritability, depression and even panic about the impending festivities which they may be looking forward to at a conscious level. In order to justify the feelings of anger and depression which they cannot understand, they may unconsciously provoke crises in their work or family relationships; they may even literally make themselves sick. Like children who have been consistently rejected and deprived of physical affection by their parents, such individuals keep themselves apart, feeling different, being stoic, standing guard over their intense desire for attachment and belonging in case it opens up another opportunity for disappointment. But like these rejected children, their hearts are pounding, their bodies registering the pain of such renunciation.

But our children give us a second chance. Even the most deprived and cynical parents feel the impulse to make Christmas special for their own children. In the service of gratifying their children's desires, they may learn to liberate their own. Though they themselves may never have experienced a really happy Christmas, they can reach back to their carefully nurtured fantasies of what it might have been and find the energy to create it for another.

Christmas, in Longfellow's description, is one of 'the secret anniversaries of the heart'. It is no wonder feelings run high at Christmas. Hope, joy, nurturance, longing, mourning, celebrating: these are big emotions, they need a big communal stage. They need rituals to give them the free expression they deserve and to safely corral the inevitable excesses and psychological consequences. Our ancestors may have done all this up on a hill, cooled by the winter moon. We have to do it in the bosom of our all too human families, in the overheated, cramped world of crowded churches, suburban homes and smoky pubs, occasionally basking, but sometimes simmering in the enforced intimacy of Christmas. The problem is not that Christmas has grown too big. Rather, it is not big enough for all we bring to it. That is why all the hype works. Nobody makes millions at Easter or Midsummer or May Day. But at Christmas we are all collectively and unconsciously ready to be whipped up into a fury of preparations, festivities and, essentially, wish fulfilment.

So, this Christmas, like all those who have gone before us, we will drink and carouse and fall on each other to keep the hope alive that once again we will be delivered from the darkness and loneliness of winter, from the fear of not being loved, and be ushered into an era of abundance. We will celebrate with plenty: the festive meal, the gathering of the clan, the riotous, defiant shouting in the dark — we are not alone in this world and we are not wanting.

Chocs, Fags, Gin and Sex, Anybody?

Traditionally the New Year is a time of resolutions for personal change. Somebody recently estimated that up to 75 per cent of Americans are either themselves 'in recovery' from some addictive behaviour or other, or know somebody who is. It is likely, then, that much of the New Year effort at personal change will be directed at traditional addictive behaviours, such as smoking, drinking and overeating or at some of the 'newer' addictions to, for example, unsuitable partners, exercise or even sex. Before you embark on your list of 'shoulds' for the New Year, it may be worth reflecting on the typical fate of such resolutions.

Relapse rates for addictive behaviours related to drinking, smoking and obesity are in the range of 50 – 90 per cent. This is a sobering finding. Why do people who want to change themselves and their behaviour fail so often? The most likely reason is that personal change is often construed as a matter of willpower, conjuring up images of self-denial and being at war with oneself. Heroic effort is followed by a lapse that is not planned for. The lapse triggers a further loss of control, followed by collapse into self-pity or self-loathing. In their anxiety to eliminate undesirable behaviour, it is understandable that people do not want to burden the enterprise with too much complexity. Yet any personal change occurs in a complex ecology of beliefs and feelings about self and others, and a sense (often unarticulated) about how the process will end.

Psychologists who study personal change are attending more and more to this ecology and less to specific techniques. Whether it is giving up cigarettes, cutting down on drink, losing weight or the emotional changes that occur in therapy, it is now clear that almost any technique works for some people, but no technique works for everybody. Rather, what is critical is developing psychological awareness of one's own emotional and behavioural patterns and learning the skills to manage the business of change.

Important insights into this process are provided by research into the phenomenon of relapse. Relapse is defined as an act of backsliding, worsening or subsiding. In other words, it is a process. Part of this process is the lapse, that is, the slight error or slip, the temporary fall, the re-emergence of a previous habit. The lapse may or may not lead to a full relapse. This is a critical distinction. When a slip is defined as temporary, a mistake, it implies that corrective action can be taken. It is the individual's response to these lapses that will determine if the programme for personal change will continue or collapse.

What determines whether an individual will interpret a lapse as a manageable mistake or a fall over a cliff from which there is no return? It seems that in that vital space between lapse and relapse self-efficacy is the key. For example, smokers who slipped (smoked at least one cigarette) and then regained abstinence attributed their slip to situational factors ('In this particular set of circumstances, my resolution was less effective. However, if I change some or all of those circumstances, I could succeed'). Those who relapsed completely after a slip blamed their own character faults ('I have no willpower').

Disappointment and frustration are apparent in everybody who lapses from a self-imposed decision to change one's personal life. However, those who have a high level of self-efficacy have a better capacity to withstand failure and show more persistence in the face of frustration. They are more able to predict and manage potential threats. Those who have a low level of self-efficacy are thrown by failure. They are more susceptible to self-doubt, dwell on their deficiencies, imagine the potential difficulties as worse than they are, rather than plan how best to proceed after a lapse. What matters is whether or not failure can be construed as a constructive experience, a way of learning more about your own patterns and how to prevent further lapses in the future.

What factors govern lapses and relapses? These can be broadly grouped into individual and interpersonal factors, situational factors and physiological factors. The first category includes stress, depression and anxiety which account for between 30 and 70 per cent of relapses. For example, in one study 71 per cent of smokers who had relapsed reported negative feelings preceding the relapse; the most common state was anxiety, followed by anger or depression. Single lapses are associated with situational factors, but relapses occur during periods of stress. Moreover, those who had originally smoked to relieve negative feelings increased the risk of a relapse.

Inadequate initial motivation is another factor that determines relapse. Change that is embarked on because of social pressure only is likely to be undermined by private resistance and unconscious defiance. Unless change is desired primarily for one's own benefit, it is not likely to last. Many change programmes are embarked on in a burst of enthusiasm, without a plan for managing the process in the longer term. Change in any aspect of behaviour may affect other aspects of life, such as personal relationships, social activities, body image, self-esteem and time management.

While early enthusiasm is critical to get started, a too rigid adherence to a programme (for example a diet) can be counterproductive. Those who have to struggle with the programme initially and who have weathered some false starts often do better in the long run than those who adhere perfectly to the programme from the beginning. Such perfectionists seem to have trouble recovering from the inevitable slip that the early perfectionism merely postponed. Again, the positive anticipation and management of failure seems to be the critical issue.

A range of strategies is important to cope with the inevitable temptations and lapses. The ability to distract oneself and to use reassuring 'self-talk' to mitigate the feelings of failure and instil confidence are particularly helpful. For those who are dieting, having a mental 'threshold' or danger signal (regaining three pounds or less) to trigger corrective action has been found to characterise the individuals who succeed in long-term weight control.

Physiological factors might be expected to manifest themselves in urges, cravings and withdrawal. Yet the results are inconsistent. Some suggest that physiological craving accounts for as little as 9 per cent of relapses in smokers, while others find that nearly half the relapses occurred in conjunction with withdrawal symptoms. In the case of dieting, the physical pressures exerted by the body to regain lost weight may be extremely powerful. For example, the number and size of fat cells, and the metabolic rate change may be related to a 'set-point' body weight which the organism defends against fluctuations, including weight loss. Yet in the over-reliance on willpower, we behave as if the body were some barrier to our 'real self', not really part of us, and our efforts to subdue and control it have much the same effect as trying to 'make' a baby stop crying from distress or hunger.

The need to include the body when trying to change addictive behaviours is underlined by the key role exercise plays in weight control, giving up smoking and dealing with alcoholism. For example, of 2,500 people who took up running, fully 81 per cent of the men and 75 per cent of the women who were smokers when they started gave up smoking shortly after.

Environmental and social factors also play a significant role in preventing relapse. Support from family and friends is one of the few factors that is associated with long-term success at losing weight, giving up smoking and stopping drinking. Conversely, 48 per cent of all relapses occur in conjunction with interpersonal stress, with one-third being caused by conflict — the opposite of social support. Thus, supportive personal relationships can help, and stressful relationships can scupper, personal change programmes.

All these factors exert an influence at different stages of the personal change process. An effective programme for personal change must deal with this complex ecology. Clearly, a high level of self-awareness and self-monitoring is required. Is there a 'safe point' before which relapse is likely and beyond which relapse is unlikely? In the case of giving up drugs, drink or cigarettes, relapse is less likely after three months, but there is no certain 'safe point'. Of smokers who gave up cigarettes on the basis of New Year's resolutions, 21 per cent were successful at the four months stage and also at the twelve months stage. This might suggest that relapse rates show a 'safe point' at the four months stage. However, different individuals formed the 21 per cent at the two stages. Some of those successful at the four month stage had relapsed by the twelve-month stage and vice versa. Although individuals may be able to identify for themselves the point of no return to the addictive behaviours, so far no reliable universal 'safe points' have been established.

But the need for continual self-awareness should not be experienced as a burden. Often it is only when people try to change their behaviour that they develop insight as to why they have ended up as the individual they are. Overeating may be masking a general tension that the person becomes aware of in themselves only when they try to diet and experience the almost unbearable tension of deciding whether or not to have another bite of food. Similarly, only when suffering the sense of profound deprivation that lack of an alcoholic drink can trigger does an individual become aware of how few other treats or comforts there are in his or her life. Much addictive-like behaviour masks problems with personal autonomy and decision-making. Unless these underlying issues and needs are attended to, it is nearly impossible to achieve desired change.

Finally, before you put your New Year resolutions into operation, it is worth looking not just at the behaviour you want to change but the underlying reason you want to change it. Unless this behavioural change will allow you to achieve an important life goal or express some quality that is now unacknowledged in your life (being free, in control, personally responsible, able to rise to a challenge), it will be difficult to create a vision of the 'new you' to sustain you through the inevitable stress, boredom and privation of personal change programmes. The goal is not to set up a process of fighting or going against yourself. Rather, it is creating the possibility of becoming more fully and truly yourself.

'In Two Places at One Time'

To discuss Irish emigration in the twentieth century, says sociology professor Liam Ryan, is virtually the same as discussing Ireland itself, since there is hardly a single political, social, economic, intellectual or religious problem which has not been directly or indirectly influenced by emigration. Emigration is at the centre of the Irish experience of being modern. We have made the transition from a traditional rural society to a modern industrial one by the simple expedient of offering a modern way of life to 75 per cent of the population and offering the remaining 25 per cent the choice of unemployment at home or migration abroad.

Seamus Heaney, addressing an Ireland Funds conference on emigration in 1989, supplied a rich theme. In Ireland, he said, we are capable of a doubleness of focus, a capacity to live in two places at the one time and in two times at the one place, a capacity to acknowledge the claims of contradictory truths without having to choose between them.

Thus, we acknowledge the historical inevitability of modernism, and all its consequences, but register that violence is being done to that more elemental sense of ourselves. Nowhere is that transition more violent and displacing for people than in emigration. But where do we register that sense of displacement and violence being done? How is the loss recorded in our collective consciousness? In our attitude to emigration, is our capacity for double focus so overused that we are paralysed by ambivalence, incapable of action?

Maurice Hayes, another contributor to that Ireland Funds conference, neatly summarised that ambivalence. We are capable, he says, of seeing emigration as a triumph or a disaster: on the one hand, the Irish taking over the world with their brains, energy, culture and Christian faith; on the other, the Irish banished from their own land by political, religious or economic oppression. Emigration is variously seen as a national haemorrhage, a failure of politics and economics or as an opportunity energetically grasped by those with 'get up and go'; as a safety valve in the social system, a way to keep unemployment and poverty at acceptable levels, to export our social misfits, or as a catastrophic loss of the young, energetic, risk-taking entrepreneurial talent that Ireland so desperately needs. Do we export our successes or our failures? Either way, what does it say about those of us left behind, how does it leave us feeling about ourselves?

In the Irish mind, emigration is the blank screen on to which we can project every unresolved issue about identity, self-confidence, past grievances and prospects for the future. It is, Joe Lee points out, the rough proxy for national success or failure.

The past 150 years have witnessed the greatest mass migration of people in world history. War, famine, persecution, the demands of advanced capitalism, the lure of a better life in a new world — all have combined to put great masses of people on the move. But by the late twentieth century, in most western countries, this mass movement had come to an end. Only in Ireland, says Liam Ryan, does it continue with a peculiar nineteenth-century intensity. The sheer scale makes it hard to comprehend. In 1988, for example, the number leaving the state (approximately 45,000) came close to the number born (54,000).

Irish emigration has a long pedigree. The million people — the 'bone and sinew' of the country — who left in the aftermath of the Great Famine, marked a change in scale in Ireland, rather than a new phenomenon. Graeme Kirkham, a historian, has documented the population movements, including the significant Protestant outflow from the north in the seventeenth and early eighteenth centuries. Prospective settlers, soldiers, adventurers, missionaries and merchants went in search of the better life. But the movement of people was sporadic, unstructured.

The Famine changed all that. Historian Kerby Miller, in his monumental work *Emigrants and Exiles,* described how the exodus in the latter half of the 1840s assumed the character of a precipitate flight, a headlong flight of panic-striken refugees, running lemming-like into the sea, away from a doomed and starving island. They were willing to take any chance — perilous voyages in disease-ridden coffin ships, destitution in North America — any chance save that of remaining in Ireland. From all sides came expressions of despair — 'Poor Ireland's done … the country's gone forever'. It was an exodus marked by what another historian has called a note of doom, an air of finality, a sense that a chapter of history had come decisively to a close. And it had, because thereafter mass emigration became institutionalised, a fact of Irish life.

But something else happened too. That catastrophic loss of trust in Ireland became institutionalised in the Irish psyche as an unconscious woundedness, a loss of confidence. Escape and avoidance became deeply ingrained as our first defence against threat.

Between the end of the Famine and the early twentieth century, Irish society tried to regroup. It faced into the developmental challenge of becoming a modern state. But our sense of woundedness cast a long shadow over the enterprise. Shaken in our confidence, the idea of modernity was approached from a culture of scarcity rather than plenty. We met the challenge to change with a frozen, anxious kiss, rather than an exuberant embrace.

According to Miller, the economic and social changes that heralded the modernisation of Ireland ushered in a new order of consolidated land holdings, impartible inheritance, the dowry system, the conversion of tillage to pasture, the introduction of labour-saving machinery. It also ushered in a new social order: an alliance of the clergy, affluent farmers and shopkeepers with a distinctly nationalist ideology, which forged a new bourgeois culture of stifling respectability, sexual repression, devotional piety, social conformity. Traditional peasant practices and attitudes, the language itself, all the rich, vibrant, intensely localised traditional local culture — what Irish speakers called *duchas* — were rapidly and traumatically unravelled by the force of the changes and their indelible association with the 'backwardness' and disaster of the preceding era.

The process of modernisation of Irish society was symbiotically linked to emigration. According to Miller, during the late nineteenth and early twentieth centuries, three out of every four Irish men and women born in that period were consigned to the emigrant ships. The particular brand of defensive modernisation we espoused depended on the exodus of the dispossessed — the non-inheriting sons and daughters, the landless peasants. The more people emigrated, the more the social fabric of rural life was eroded. Already depopulated by the Famine, the silence and emptiness of the countryside engendered isolation and depression. Floods of letters and money from those who had left made America in particular seem like an appealing alternative, a second 'native land'.

The development of capitalism, depending as it did on the emergence of individual advancement, often to the obvious disadvantage of others in the same family and community, was a potential source of serious and destabilising tension within families and communities. It also came into conflict with prevailing Catholic world-views, which stressed the value of solidarity rather than individualism, tradition versus innovation, conformity versus initiative, fatalism versus optimism, passivity versus action, dependence versus independence. Our capacity for double focus came into its own.

The troublesome notions of the economic betterment of the few being dependent on the mass emigration of the dispossessed, or indeed of emigration to better oneself, were masked and brought into harmony with the imagined Ireland, although the imagining was defensive, constricted. Miller argues that we opted for the notion of emigration as involuntary exile, *deorai* — outside the control of individuals or the society, brought about by fate, or more usually by British oppression or Protestant ascendancy. The powerful defence mechanism of escape was now overladen with the equally powerful feelings of victimisation and passive destiny.

Although Irish society was at one level responding to the exigencies and opportunities of capitalism, our ambivalence forced us to obscure or excuse such individualism. The Catholic clergy, according to Miller, played a pivotal role. Caught between the demands of the poor that they support radical measures to halt emigration and the demands of the affluent that they do no such thing, the Catholic clergy formulated an ideological explanation of emigration that squared the circle. The idealised, semi-mythical idea of Holy Ireland, a kind of fortress Hibernia, which was brought into play, had to be continually defended against external assault and internal conflict.

Holy Ireland was conceptualised as indifferent to the false gods of modernism and materialism. Because of such unworldliness, the Irish were profoundly conservative, content to live simple lives. To ensure such continuity and stability, Holy Ireland's economy had to remain agriculturally based, socially rooted in the devout and traditional peasant family. Such a society, of course, left no place for the non-inheriting sons and daughters of landless peasants, but it allowed the clergy and the nationalists to oppose emigration and condemn the emigrants themselves for deserting their posts, intolerably weakening the ranks, selfishly repudiating Mother Ireland.

In a masterly account, Kerby Miller describes how the American wake served not just as a poignant goodbye from family and friends but as a communal ritual to lament departures, not to extol the emigrant as an ambitious or carefree individual, but rather to impress upon the hapless emigrant the full burden of grief, filial duty, obligation and self-abnegation as the price of departure. The songs and lamentations served to reproach the emigrant with how lonely and bereft the parents would be and to remind them of the everlasting debt they owed the parents who had reared them. At their moment of greatest vulnerability — their traumatic expulsion from childhood intimacies and sense of belonging — their initiation into adulthood was used powerfully to reinforce their obligations to family and country.

When children have to rely on parents who are themselves too emotionally needy and preoccupied to care properly for them, when they are constantly reminded of how many sacrifices are being made for them and are blamed for being 'too demanding' and being distressed, they develop what psychologists call an anxious-ambivalent attachment style. They become preoccupied with the parent, full of resentment and anger, yet clingy and anxious for reunion. They become confused about their own motivation, uncertain about their perception of reality. Many emigrants, confronted with the stress of separation, develop a similar syndrome.

The emigrants who went to England, says Liam Ryan, thought of Ireland as their home, where they really belonged, a place to which they might return one day. They nurtured images and memories of laughing crowds and sunny evenings. But when they returned, they found it to be a different place. They longed for England again, only to find that there too was disappointment. Caught up in confused memories and myths, they could never accept the reality in either country. Mary Corcoran, in her superb study of the young Irish illegals in New York, found the same ambivalence. This was expressed in the highly dichotomised views that the emigrants constructed of Ireland and America, idealising one then another, swinging constantly between love and hate, longing and disappointment. She observed that while new emigrants roundly criticised the old Irish-Americans for myth-making, they themselves were busy constructing a mythic 'traditional' Ireland that was largely an artefact of the past.

Just as the old emigrants were shaped into seeing themselves as exile-victims of British political oppression, the new emigrants were busy psychologically transforming the economic and social act of emigration into a different kind of mythic exile. They borrowed the new ideology underpinning emigration, seeing themselves as new-age carpet-baggers: highly skilled, inner-directed, robust entrepreneurs and adventurers who could not be contained within the confines of national boundaries. 'We cannot all live on one small island, we have too much to offer the world' proclaims one of the new Irish in Corcoran's study. They believed too, like many of the old emigrants, that it was a temporary exile. The boundless talent, tempered and perfected by experience abroad, eventually will return to Ireland. The reality, of course, as Mary Corcoran points out, is that only a small number fall into that category and those that do are unlikely to return once they have experienced the rewards abroad.

And what of those left behind? It seems inevitable that all the ambivalence emigrants feel about leaving and we feel about being left makes us unsettled. We are, in Seamus Heaney's phrase, vaguely in exile from somewhere inside or outside ourselves, though we don't quite know how or why. It is as if the psychological transformations from native to emigrant of the millions who left impinge on our notions of ourselves, on our centre of gravity. We take on their heightened sense of Irishness-in-exile even before we go. We can stand in an Irish pub, singing the songs of exile with the same poignancy as if we had already left. We bend to our destiny before it even calls. We identify readily with a romantic notion of diaspora. But unlike the Jewish people who had physically lost their homeland, we simply do not feel securely at home here. So many have gone, and continue to go, that the sheer energy of their absence acts like a magnetic field.

We are riveted too by the fact that for all their ambivalence, in that strange space between two cultures, the emigrants could exhibit a productivity and doggedness that rarely surfaced at home. Liam Ryan's study of the Irish in Britain provided an unforgettable description of the 'Paddies', the vast army of the unskilled who literally built modern Britain. It was a description matched by Mary Corcoran's depiction of the new Irish illegals in New York. They too worked from dawn to dusk, eagerly embracing a work ethic where personal advancement and making an honest buck were more important than adhering to petty class snobberies and distinctions between white- or blue-collar jobs. These young people wryly note that they take jobs abroad that their parents would never allow them to take at home. Perhaps that is why we have failed to produce the entrepreneurial talent that might transform the economy and produce jobs. Instead, a study in 1971 noted that, while in that same year there were 4,000 Irish-born doctors and dentists and 31,000 nurses, there were in Ireland itself only 3,500 doctors and 19,000 nurses.

If emigration has taught us anything, it is that we have a supply of dammed-up energy just waiting to be released. But first, in this year commemorating the 150th anniversary of the Famine, we must relinquish our politics of scarcity and make an act of faith in ourselves. We shall have to move confidently into a sense of Irishness that can sustain a vision of abundance, that can at least imagine the island as big, generous and inclusive enough to sustain us all. Our Irishness, Heaney writes, 'constitutes a big unconscious voltage and all it needs is some transformer to make it current in a new and significant and renovative way'. This, in turn, could form 'the emotional structure of a modern, creative, patriotic action'. To construct that transformer is all our business.

Index